May Bell's Daughter

Eva Whittington Self
with Lisa Harper

T0321505

THOMAS NELSON PUBLISHERS®
Nashville

Published in Nashville, Tennessee, by Thomas Nelson, Inc.

Unless otherwise noted, Scripture quotations are from THE NEW KING JAMES VERSION. Copyright © 1979, 1980, 1982, Thomas Nelson, Inc., Publishers.

Scripture quotations noted KJV are from the KING JAMES VERSION. Scripture quotations noted TLB are from *The Living Bible*, copyright © 1971. Used by permission of Tyndale House Publishers, Inc., Wheaton, Illinois 60189. All rights reserved.

Scripture quotations noted NIV are taken from the HOLY BIBLE, NEW INTERNATIONAL VERSION ®. Copyright © 1973, 1978, 1984 by International Bible Society. Used by permission of Zondervan Bible Publishing House. All rights reserved.

The "NIV" and "New International Version" trademarks are registered in the United States Patent and Trademark Office by International Bible Society. Use of either trademark requires the permission of International Bible Society.

Library of Congress Cataloging-in-Publication Data

Self, Eva Whittington.
   May Bell's daughter / Eva Whittington Self.
     p. cm.
     ISBN 13: 978-1-59555-227-3
     1. Self, Eva Whittington—Health. 2. Paraplegics—North
Carolina Biogrtaphy. 3. Physically handicapped women—North
Carolina Biography. I. Title.
    RC406.P3S45 1999
    362.4'3'092—dc21
    [B]   99-20415
                                         CIP

Published in the United States of America

1 2 3 4 5 6 BVG 04 03 02 01 00 99

To Our Daughters
Abby and Audrey

Only be careful, and watch yourselves closely so that you do not forget the things your eyes have seen or let them slip for your heart as long as you live. Teach them to your children and to their children after them.

Deut. 4:9 NIV

$\mathcal{C}$ontents

CONTENTS

$\mathcal{A}$cknowledgments

I have never written a book before. I never dreamed that I would write a book, much less be the subject of a book. It has been an exciting, challenging, and humbling process. It has been both enjoyable and painful to relive my life's experiences as we have written this book.

This book is the result of contributions by a lot of significant people. I'd like to tell you about a few of them:

Thanks to my dear friend and co-author, Lisa Harper, who first asked me to pray about writing a book five years ago. Her vision, encouragement, and gracious persistence have led to this project becoming a reality. I pray that her heart's desire to glorify God and minister to women will be fulfilled by this book.

Thanks to Mike Hyatt at Thomas Nelson who convinced me that my story was worth telling, not only at large conferences and in small churches, but also in written form. Mike's wise counsel and professionalism helped reassure me that this was a project worth doing. He helped us to not only do it, but to do it well.

To my Sunday school class at First Baptist, Hopkinsville and the Sims/DeWeese Bible study for their constant encouragement and prayers. Thanks to Barbara Sledd for the long walks and meaningful talks.

Thanks to my husband's secretary, Rita Black, for all the typing, shipping, handling, faxing, and everything else. Thanks especially, for retyping parts of the manuscript (sorry we made you cry).

Thanks to my in-laws, Dr. Ben and Carolyn Self, for all their prayers, encouragement, support, and for being on-call grandparents.

Thanks to my husband, Andrew, who is my ghostwriter, editor, agent, and, of course, my lawyer. He is my personal trainer and motivator. He knows when to push and when to pull. He is my balance and my estrogen neutralizer, especially when I . . . well, you know. He is the best father my girls could ever have. He is my best friend and partner for life.

$\mathcal{I}$ntroduction

Summers are hot in North Carolina. Real hot. And real humid. Because we never had air-conditioning in the small five-room house where my mama and daddy raised my five older brothers and me—Daddy thought air-conditioning was bad for a person—the only relief we could get from the heat was to find a shade tree or a porch swing. Fortunately, we had both.

I was raised in Concord, just outside Charlotte. Both Mama and Daddy worked in textile mills. Mama had worked the first shift at Cannon Mills from the time she was sixteen years old. Daddy worked the third shift and either played or umpired baseball most of his life. Where I came from, baseball, the mill, and the church were the three main ingredients in life—sometimes in that order.

In the summer of 1980, when I was only nineteen years old, I was invited to speak at the North Carolina Youth Evangelism Conference in Greensboro. It was being held in the Greensboro Coliseum and the organizers were expecting five thousand people. I'm not sure I had ever seen five thousand people in one place before, let alone spoken to them. I was excited, but very nervous.

It helped to know that my home church, Southside Baptist, was bringing a busload of young people to the conference for moral support. My friend Donna Mac and I had already left for the conference the day before. But the one person I hoped would be there—really, the only person I needed to be there other than the Lord—was my mama, May Bell Whittington.

Mama didn't drive, so I knew she'd either have to get Daddy to bring her, which was unlikely, or she would have to catch a ride with somebody else. Because Greensboro was almost two hours away from home, I really didn't think Mama would be able to make it. So I did what she had taught me time and time again to do in those kinds of situations. I prayed. All day long as I prayed, I imagined what was taking place at home.

Because it was summertime, I knew that Mama had spent at least part of the day out in the garden picking tomatoes. I could see her cradling the tomatoes against her chest with one arm while the other moved her Lucky Strike cigarette back and forth from her mouth to her side.

I knew that if Mama was going to make it to the conference, she'd have to fix Daddy an early supper, probably of fresh pinto beans, tomatoes, and some bread. She'd have to tell him over and over again that his food was ready. There were at least two reasons for that: one, Daddy couldn't hear very well, and two, the baseball game on TV would be turned up way too loud.

After Mama had taken care of Daddy, she would take care of herself. No doubt she would have her best red dress all laid out on the bed, inside out, and before she changed into it, she'd sprinkle baby powder all over it. She'd then put baby powder on her as the sweat continued to roll down her face.

After Mama finished dressing, she'd get down on her

knees beside the bed and pray. She'd stay there for several minutes, praying for both me and Daddy. I've walked in on her so many times when she was on her knees by her bed that I could clearly picture her in my mind.

When Mama finished praying, she'd straighten herself, smooth her dress, put on bright red lipstick, and walk in to tell Daddy she was ready to go.

While I was getting ready to speak in Greensboro, I could imagine all of this so clearly, but what I didn't know was that Mama had already arranged for a ride to Greensboro. Mama was determined to be there for me and she wasn't going to miss it for anything.

One of my friends from church came by that afternoon to pick up Mama so that she could ride the church bus with the youth group. My friend also tried to talk Daddy into coming along. A Youth Evangelism Conference sounded too much like church to him so he decided to stay home and watch the house. Even though we didn't have much of anything, Daddy always thought somebody was trying to steal from us. So he decided to stay home and look out for all the crooks. He told Mama to watch out for the "immigrants"—what he really was trying to say was "idiots"—on the road between home and Greensboro. (Daddy often got his words confused.)

I was so proud and thankful to see Mama sitting in the audience. I told several stories about her that night, so when I closed my talk, I asked her to stand. As Mama slowly and somewhat awkwardly stood up, something neither of us expected happened. Almost as one person, the audience also rose to its feet and gave Mama a warm ovation.

For my mama to experience that was priceless. You see, throughout Mama's life, she gave a whole lot more love than she ever received. Rarely, if ever, did I hear Daddy, a member of Mama's family, or anybody else offer any encouragement or support to Mama. But that never stopped her from loving or giving or serving others.

If you had ever met my mama, you would probably have come away saying that she was not half as pretty on the outside as she was on the inside. To others, May Bell Whittington might not have seemed like anything more than a backward country girl, a mill worker, or a housewife. But to me, my mama was the greatest evangelist who ever lived. For you see, while I was at a very young age my mama introduced me to Jesus Christ. And she introduced me to Him in such a way that I knew He would always be there with me in the good times and the bad.

My name is Eva. I'm May Bell's daughter. This story is as much hers as it is mine.

1

pecial!

Freely you have received, freely give.
(Matthew 10:8)

grew up in a family that made me feel special. From the time I was born I knew that I was special for several reasons. I was the first girl born into the Whittington family in more than a hundred years. There were also five boys who grew up in the family before me. My next older brother was seven years old when I was born, so I am the "baby" and I am a girl. It's hard to get more special than that.

I was definitely a number–one, grade-A, government-inspected "Daddy's girl." My daddy always knew how to make me feel special. Especially later in my life when I came home from college, he knew the time I would arrive and he'd be sitting on the back steps of our house. He'd jump up and run toward the car, waving both of his hands over his head and shouting, "Hey, hey, oh boy, oh boy." I'd just hope the neighbors weren't looking! He'd help me out of the car, push me up the ramp to my bedroom, and all over my bed, from head to foot, I'd find chewing gum and candy. I was always very popular in the dorm at college after a visit home!

My brothers also had ways of making me feel "special." I feel certain that my brothers would lie awake at night thinking of all the "special" things they could do for their "special" little sister when Mama and Daddy weren't at home—none of which I thought were very special at all. Being the baby meant being the brunt of a lot of practical jokes. And, in case you ever have any doubts about it, no matter who tells you to lick a metal ice-cube tray on a hot summer's day . . . don't do it.

If you were born into my family, you were an athlete. You were either a good athlete or a bad athlete—but you were an athlete. There was no way around it. I learned about competition early in my life.

Daddy often said to me, "Eva, if you want to be good in sports, you've got to get in there and compete with the boys." I'd say back to him, "Daddy, I compete with these fellas for everything."

Have you ever had to compete for time in the bathroom with boys? I have never understood what takes them so long in the bathroom. They can spend hours behind a locked door but when they emerge, they look just the same as when they walked in! At least when women spend time in front of a bathroom mirror they come out looking different.

When my older brothers came to Sunday dinner, I knew that I'd better have one hand on a bowl of something during the blessing because before the "Amen" quit echoing in the room, my brothers would be eating. And they could put away food!

My brothers were all good athletes so the level of competition in our family was usually pretty intense. One of the games we enjoyed playing when I was a child was called "Peggie." We had big-time Peggie games on Sunday afternoons at the go-cart track behind our garden. I felt I had really arrived when the boys allowed me to play Peggie with them.

Just about everything we did around the house was done in an athletic, competitive way. Even if we were folding towels, we turned it into a game of fun. One of my brothers created a game called "Rag Fight" and there were times when I realized that if I hadn't been coordinated, I might easily have been killed in the normal course of "play."

Any athletic ability I got came from Daddy. Mama was *not* an athlete. In fact, she wasn't the least bit coordinated.

Neither was Mama very musical. Daddy had a great voice and my brother and I grew up loving to sing the songs Daddy taught us and that we learned at Sunday school. Mama couldn't sing a lick—in fact, she couldn't carry a tune.

She was still very special to me.

Mama helped raise four boys before she had my brother and me. Those four boys weren't hers—in fact, two of them weren't even my daddy's. My father's first wife abandoned Daddy and her sons and later, Daddy and Mama took in two boys whose parents had divorced and had sent them out to find homes of their own. Mama helped raise those boys and my brother with the same love and care she raised me. I love her for that.

Mama didn't have any real physical beauty that would have attracted people to her. She was tall and lanky and later in her life, she had a little pot-belly. Once a year she went down the street to a neighbor's beauty shop and got a permanent, but most of the time she wore her hair short and she fixed it the best she could. She wore bright red lipstick when she went to church, but she wasn't a beautiful woman.

Neither was my mama very stylish. Mostly I remember her wearing polyester pantsuits around the house because they were comfortable. She made most of her clothes as a way to save money. She wore simple dresses to church.

In spite of all these outward appearances and traits, there was something very special inside my mama that made her different. She passed that "something" on to me. Mama introduced me to Jesus.

Mama knew Jesus in such a way that I *knew* who He was. I knew He was not only the God who lived beyond the hills and beyond the stars and the clouds—He was a God who could live inside my own heart and always be there for me. I knew He was someone I could always call a Friend.

Mama may not have traveled to all the places I've been. She didn't have the opportunity to shake the hands of all the people I've met. But her influence and testimony live on because of her faith that she passed on to me.

Mama also taught me that every person is special and that the Lord has a special job for every person that walks on the earth. By her life more than any one thing she said, Mama showed me that the most important thing a person can ever do is introduce someone to Jesus. She showed me that whatever the Lord has taught you, pass it on—not in a way that offends people, but in your normal conversation and in the way you live your life.

There's nothing more special than growing up with a Christian mama. She gave me roots and she gave me wings. She taught me what it means to give freely, and to never stop giving. She taught me how to love God.

2

Growing up on Linden Avenue

"For the oppression of the poor,
for the sighing of the needy,
Now I will arise," says the LORD;
"I will set him in the safety for
which he yearns."
(Psalm 12:5)

We lived on Linden Avenue, right across the street from Calvary Foursquare Church. That little white, wooden church across the street from us had a church yard in which I played and it had a long cement sidewalk leading up to the front steps—a perfect place for dribbling basketballs. When I sat on those church steps, I had a good view of the entire street. In many ways, it was a view of my entire world.

We had a neighborhood store where we could buy candy and Cokes. It was actually a house converted into a store and it was something of a gathering place for people in our neighborhood. The rest of the neighborhood was houses.

Our house on Linden Avenue was my favorite house on the block. It was just a small house with two bedrooms and one bathroom, but I was proud that we didn't have a broken-down car or any old furniture sitting in our front yard like most of the other houses. A number of houses in my neighborhood still had outhouses when I was growing up. Wringer-style washing machines and tin bathtubs were common. I was proud that we had indoor plumbing. We also had a chain-link fence around our yard, and we had flower boxes. For me, it was a safe and happy place to grow up.

In reality, it wasn't all that safe or all that happy—but Mama *made* my life safe and happy.

We were poor when I was a child. Although I knew we were poor, I didn't really know what being poor meant.

A boy named Bobby Dale made fun of my shoes in the fourth grade—he called them "grandma shoes." I went home and told Mama about it and she said she wished she could buy me new shoes but we didn't have the money for them. When Bobby Dale made fun of my shoes the next day, I told him to quit making fun of me because Mama said we didn't have enough money to buy new shoes. He never picked on me after that, at least not about being poor. If being poor meant that I didn't have a certain kind of shoes . . . well, that was really no big deal to me.

Mostly what I knew was that we weren't on welfare. Mama and Daddy both had jobs at large Cannon Mills plants in the greater Concord area. Mama folded sheets on the first shift at Plant 1 in Kannapolis, and Daddy was a slubber hand on the night shift. (Slubbers were the workers who kept the cotton threads spinning correctly on the huge looms.)

Since Daddy worked at the mill at night, Mama was always very aware that she was alone in the house with two children, no phone, and neighbors who were sometimes rowdy. Our neighbors on both sides were on welfare and we always knew when the welfare checks showed up because that night both sets of neighbors usually got drunk.

One hot summer night these neighbors got really loud in their carrying on. The two families began yelling at each other across our chain-link fence in the front yard. Mostly they were threatening each other: "If you don't do so and so, we'll see that your welfare check is cut off!" They were making so much noise that we couldn't sleep.

Mama took a shotgun and after she had turned on the front porch light, she went out into the yard, fired that gun in the air, and said to both sets of stunned neighbors, "If you don't let some working people sleep, ain't nobody going to get no welfare check!"

They immediately backed down, saying, "We'll be quiet, Miss May, we'll be quiet."

Another time a drunk came to our screen door at night. He didn't seem to want to leave. Mama walked into the living room with a pellet gun and said, "Can I help you?"

"No, ma'am, no, I don't need no help," he said as he staggered back off the porch. "I'm at the wrong house!"

I felt safe with Mama at home.

Daddy came home from work every morning right before we got up. Many mornings I woke to the smell of grits, bacon, and eggs, and the sound of Daddy whistling. If we were slow in getting dressed, he'd bang a cast-iron frying pan and say, "Rise and shine, it's coffee time!"

Neither Mama nor Daddy finished high school—in fact, Mama only made it through the sixth grade and Daddy through the fourth grade. But just as I didn't know we were poor when I was a child, I didn't know my parents were uneducated. I just knew that they worked hard at the mill, Daddy was usually around in the morning, and Mama came home in the afternoon in time to fix supper. And I knew that we ate a lot of potatoes—fried potatoes, stewed potatoes, mashed potatoes—and every so often, we had meat with the potatoes.

Now that I'm an adult, I know how hard it must have been for Mama to raise six children with very little money, holding down a full-time, physically demanding job all those years. I know how much she must have wanted to stay home with her children. But Mama did work. In fact, at six o'clock every morning, she walked about a half mile to the end of Linden Avenue to take a bus that would take her several miles away to Kannapolis where Plant 1 was located. At the plant, she stood all day folding sheets. At the end of the day, she made the trip home. Before Mama left for work in the mornings, she'd come and kiss my brother and me good-bye. Many mornings I arrived at school with lipstick still on my cheek. Mama may not have *wanted* to work in the mill, but she did what she knew she needed to do.

Mama was very resourceful. She made good use of everything made available to her. The sewing room was right beside the folding room at Plant 1, and many times the sewers would have scraps. Mama occasionally brought home sheets or sheet scraps and she made summer clothes for me out of the fabric. I always thought the things she made were cute. It never dawned on me I was wearing sheets! I was simply wearing clothes that Mama made—clothes that were comfortable for summertime play.

Most of my happy childhood memories seem to be "summer memories." We went fishing in the summer. We had a very large vegetable garden in the backyard and that garden produced a great deal of the food we ate all year. What we didn't eat fresh in the summer, we canned for use in the winter. We gave away a lot of vegetables to the neighbors, too. Daddy could grow the best tomatoes in the world.

We'd go to the beach over the Fourth of July weekend because the mill shut down then. Daddy and his buddies would go deep-sea fishing and we'd go to the boardwalk. We always brought home the fish and had fish all year. In fact, every Friday night we ate fish. On the way home from the beach, we'd stop for a picnic lunch of tomato sandwiches—tomatoes, salt and pepper, mayonnaise, and white bread.

When we weren't doing chores or working in the garden, we played games, or we'd "sit and sing." Daddy and all my brothers had good singing voices. I learned dozens of songs growing up, and got pretty good at singing harmony, too.

We also played a lot of baseball.

My father was a baseball player. In fact, you could hardly have a conversation with Daddy unless you knew something about baseball. He played professionally in what was called the Carolina Baseball League before he and Mama married. He was an outfielder and a catcher, but mostly he was known as a great home-run hitter. Just about everybody in the area knew about Shad Whittington.

Daddy's real name was James, and Mama called him Jim, but to everybody else he was Shad. It was a nickname he acquired because once when he came to bat, the out-fielder on the opposite team said, "I think I'll just sit down in the shade." He fully expected Daddy to hit a home run and he thought he'd take a little rest while Daddy rounded the bases. The other players began to call Daddy the Shade Man, which was shortened to Shad.

Daddy took care of me during the day and we often went down to Hipp-McBrides, a sporting goods store where Daddy and some of his friends gathered regularly. I remember that the floors of that store were oiled—they always looked a little greasy to me. I couldn't sit on the floor so the owner would bring out a fold-up fishing stool for me to sit on while Daddy told his stories. The men would stand around for an hour or more, saying to Daddy, "Tell us another one, Shad!"

I felt pretty special being the only girl in the group, and especially because I got to drink a Coke *out of the bottle!*

Most of Daddy's stories were about baseball. He'd do the sound effects and use various voices and imitate the roar

13

of the crowd. I can still hear his voice as he'd tell about hitting a ball so far that he made it look like an "azburn" tablet—meaning an aspirin tablet.

Daddy loved to tell stories. It didn't matter if people had heard a story before—Daddy still loved to tell it, and people still seemed to enjoy listening to it. Over the years, some of the stories got more and more colorful.

I got my love for telling stories from Daddy—the only difference is that I try hard to keep my facts straight each time I tell a story!

My days with Daddy and my nights with Mama were secure. But Friday and Saturday nights were another story. At those times, my childhood became dark, dangerous, and tense.

3

The Dark Side

Behold, to obey is better than sacrifice.
(1 Samuel 15:22)

*D*addy was a character. He could be kind and loving, but he could also be a mean old man, especially when he had alcohol in him. Even after he stopped drinking, he was what some people call a "dry alcoholic"—angry and abusive in his speech, unable to stop his ranting and raving.

When I was only about four or five years old, Daddy, Mama, my brother, and I were going to my uncle's house. Daddy had been drinking and he and Mama got into a fight about his drinking and driving. He began to yell at Mama and without warning, he backhanded her over and over, four or five times. I could see that there was blood all over her face as Mama looked back at my brother as if to say, "Don't let Eva see this." My brother reached over and hugged me to shield my eyes.

Mama kept telling Daddy, "Stop the car. Let us out." He finally pulled over and we got out. Daddy, however, wanted me to stay with him so he got out of the car and grabbed me and put me back into the car. Mama refused to leave me alone with him, so she and my brother finally got back into the car and Daddy drove us home. He then drove away with a roar.

All of this was very confusing to me, but also very vivid and very real. I knew something was wrong. That night, Mama put us to bed but she insisted that we keep our clothes and shoes on. She said, "If I say, 'Let's go,' you have to get up fast and leave the house with me."

When Daddy got home, he had a fifth of liquor in his hand and he told her, "I'm going to drink all this and when I get done I'm going to smash this bottle in the kitchen sink and then I'm going to take that broken bottle and fix your face with it."

Mama yelled, "Young 'uns, get up"—and we did! I remember how the screen slammed behind us as we left the house. We walked across the street to the pastor's home beside the church and knocked on the door. The pastor answered the door and Mama asked, "Can I use your phone to call my brother?"

The pastor said, "I don't want to get involved in this."

She said, "All I'm asking is to use your phone."

He said again, "I just don't want to get involved"—and he closed the door in our faces. Mama answered through the door, "May God have mercy on your soul, man."

Mama didn't know where to turn so we began to walk around the block. I had four or five baby dolls in my arms as we walked so it was a bit of a struggle for me. We walked until Mama could think clearly enough to remember where a pay phone was located. She called her brother and he came and picked us up. We drove to the police station and Mama filed a warrant for Daddy's arrest. The police could hardly believe it was Shad Whittington who had beaten and threatened his wife in this way, but with my brother and I innocently confirming the truth of Mama's story, they had little choice but to arrest Daddy. We went to live at my grandparents' house for a few weeks while he was in jail.

After Daddy was released, he went to the mill and after Mama's shift ended, he met Mama at the gate to the mill. He got down on his knees and told Mama repeatedly how sorry he was for what he had done and he promised her he would never hit her or threaten her again if she'd come back to him. At the time, all Mama said to him was, "I'm sorry, too."

While she was trying to decide whether to return to

Daddy or to try to make a life for herself and my brother and me on her own, she heard a preacher say as part of a sermon, "Sometimes you need to put wheels on your prayers. You have to do what God has told you to do."

Mama decided that she didn't believe in divorce and that her children needed a father, so she decided she would go back to Daddy. When Mama told my grandfather that she was going back to Daddy, he said, "I never thought my daughter May Bell would take this kind of treatment or return to a man who hurt her. I'll be disappointed if you take any more of this kind of abuse."

She said, "I won't take any more of it, I promise."

I think one of the reasons my grandfather was so surprised at Mama's decision to go back to Daddy was because my mother had suffered abuse as a teenager—and she had stood against those who hurt her.

Prior to marrying Daddy, Mama dated a man for several years. They had planned to marry, but then one night when Mama was nineteen years old, she was raped by a cousin and his friend. After they had abused her, they threw her into the front yard of her parent's house.

Mama filed charges against the two young men. The day before they went to trial, my grandmother said she didn't want to go to court because she believed Mama had brought the incident on herself. My grandfather asked her, "Did you do anything to lead these boys on?" Mama said, "No, I didn't." My grandfather said, "That's all I need to hear." He supported her fully in her filing charges and in her court case.

The two men were convicted and went to prison. But Mama's fiancé didn't want anything to do with her after she had been raped.

My grandfather knew how brave my mama had been in

filing rape charges—in a time when many rape victims didn't take such action. He knew she had overcome the criticism of her own mother, and that she had also overcome the rejection of her boyfriend. Grandpa knew my mama was a courageous woman, not one to back down in tough times, and that she had no tolerance for being mistreated or abused. He was a little baffled, I think, at Mama's decision to return to Daddy after he had hurt her.

Nevertheless, Mama went back to Daddy and to the best of my knowledge, he never hit her again or did anything to hurt her physically. He still yelled and screamed, and filled the house with tension in his rages, but he didn't injure Mama physically.

I respect Mama for what she did. I'm not sure I could have done it. I don't necessarily admire her for returning to Daddy—in fact, there were lots of times through the years when I wondered if our lives might have been better if Mama had not returned to live in that house. What I admire is this: Mama did what she believed the Lord told her to do. She acted on the conviction of her heart and her entire motivation was to obey the Lord. I admire her willingness to obey the Lord even though what He asked of her was difficult.

For some women, returning to an abusive husband may not be what the Lord asks of them. Mama believed, however, that the Lord was asking her to return to Daddy as an act of her own faith. She returned to Daddy trusting that the Lord was going to do something good in Daddy's life, in our lives, and in the end, in her own life. She returned solely out of obedience to the Lord.

Mama's obedience was better than sacrifice—in lots of ways, it *was* a sacrifice of her own will, her own desire, and her own need for physical security.

4

A Song on Sunday Mornings

*Do not sorrow, for the joy
of the Lord is your strength.
(Nehemiah 8:10)*

*M*ama may have had a hard life, but on the other hand, she had the greatest asset any person can have: she knew the Lord. I never had a moment's doubt about that.

Mama couldn't sing very well but on Sunday mornings, she always seemed to be singing as she made breakfast. I think her favorite song was, "What a Friend We Have in Jesus."

Sundays were special. Every other day of the week we had grits, bacon or sausage, and eggs for breakfast. On Sunday we had rice, pork chops, and eggs. Sunday lunch was also a special meal, and at that meal, we were usually joined by my older brothers and their families.

Between breakfast and lunch we went to church. That is, Mama, my brother, and I went to church. The only times we didn't go to church were those rare occasions when Mama had to work overtime at the mill on Sundays. Then, the women at the mill would have church as they worked. While they folded sheets, someone would give a testimony or the women would sing hymns. Sunday wasn't Sunday for Mama unless there was church.

Even though there was a church right across the street from us, we went to the Methodist Church quite a ways from our house. All of Daddy's baseball buddies had families in this church so Mama believed that if Daddy ever went to any church, it would be that one. She herself had been raised in a Lutheran church but denominations never really mattered much to Mama.

Our Methodist church seemed really big to me as a

child. I remember the brick on its outside and the wooden altar rail at the front of the church sanctuary. The church had stained glass windows all around—at the back was a window of Jesus the Good Shepherd and at the front was a scene with Jesus and Peter, James, and John in the Garden of Gethsemane.

I always enjoyed Sunday school. I also loved singing in church and I always tried to sing as loud as I could. Mama seemed real proud when people would turn around and tell me I had a good voice.

After church, I looked forward to getting gum from the Chewing Gum Man who stood in the back of the church and gave chewing gum to the children. I have no idea what that man's name was, but I believe every church should have a Chewing Gum Man!

We didn't have a phone and Mama never learned to drive a car; so if Mrs. Troutman didn't come to pick us up, we walked to church. Usually somebody from the church would see us as they drove by so we rarely had to walk the entire way. Sometimes, but not very often, Daddy would drive us to church. Sometimes, he would be in the parking lot with the car when we came out of church. On those occasions, Mama was thrilled. She was happy just to see him on church property!

Both my brother and I went through confirmation class and were baptized in the church. In the summers, we hit all of the vacation Bible schools that we could—four or five, sometimes, regardless of denomination.

Mama didn't know a lot about life, but knowing the Lord was all she *needed* to know. Her faith was everything to her. She believed that God would honor her obedience and her commitment to Him.

The only thing that was as consistently important to Mama as church was praying. It was Mama who taught me about the power of prayer.

Every night, Mama would kneel by her bed and pray. It was a nightly ritual that always upset my father.

Mama didn't hurry her prayers and after she had been in the bedroom a while on her knees, Daddy would sometimes say, "What's she doing in there?" I'd say, "She's talking to God about *you*, Daddy." That would make him even more nervous.

He'd say, "I wish she'd quit that." But she didn't.

Mama didn't pray for show. Praying was just something she did every night before she went to bed. It was part of her life, part of who she was. I learned to pray because she was my *example,* and because she taught me to pray for myself.

Mama didn't pray over me or for me as much as she encouraged me to pray. If I said to her, "Mama, I'm scared tonight," Mama would say, "Eva, just talk to Jesus." I wonder sometimes if we do the right thing when we pray for people or say to them, "Well, I'll pray for you" rather than encourage them to talk to Jesus for themselves.

I believe that if I have a quiet time every day with the Lord, reading His Word and trying to listen to Him with my heart and not my head, He can reveal to me what I am supposed to do, and when and how I'm supposed to do it.

There's no one method or Bible study approach or ritual that's *the* way to hear from the Lord. Spending time with the Lord—opening up the heart to the Lord—that's the way to hear from the Lord.

Mama never went to a Bible study, at least not that I know about. She didn't read the latest books on how to do various things. She just lived her life and trusted the Lord to guide her every step of the way and to take care of her. Is life really any more complicated than that? We can make it more complicated, but do we really gain anything? I doubt it.

With the Word of God in your heart, and a relationship with the Lord in which you can talk to Him about anything and listen to Him when He speaks, you can make it through anything. I know. Mama did.

5

Dreaming Big Dreams

*For I know the thoughts that I think toward you,
says the Lord, thoughts of peace and not of evil,
to give you a future and a hope.
(Jeremiah 29:11)*

Mama taught me about dreaming dreams. She said to me, "Eva, honey, you've got to dream big dreams—really big dreams—because if you're willing to work hard enough and wait long enough, and if Jesus lives in your dreams, your dreams will live."

I took my mama's word on that and I dreamed big dreams, but most of them had been fulfilled by the time I was a senior in high school. As an all-American tomboy, I had dreamed of being on the girls' basketball team—and I was. I had dreamed of being a cheerleader—and I was. On the weekends, I coached a basketball team and taught a cheerleading squad. I was in school plays and sang in the choir and in the county ensemble. My life was full.

I also had a part-time job from six to ten in the evening at Zayre's Department Store. I was so busy in high school that I wasn't home a great deal. When I look back, it seems I was only home long enough to change clothes.

We went to a lot of ball games—softball games, baseball games, and tournaments on weekends. My brother was a great pitcher, so we especially went to a lot of his softball games. Daddy often was an umpire for those games. The newspaper ran a picture one time that was captioned "Whole Family at Plate" because one of my brothers was catching, another was at bat, and Daddy was the umpire.

When I was a sophomore in high school, I began dating a guy who worked in the mill on the second shift. He was several years older than I—in fact, he was one of my brother's best friends. He came to our house every night after work and I fixed him a deviled egg sandwich and we'd sit and talk and watch TV together.

We were planning to get married right after I graduated from high school so we talked a lot about our future together.

In my hometown, girls like me who didn't get scholarships or couldn't afford to go to college got a job right after they finished high school, and then they got married, and after a couple of years, they had babies. That was my plan. I think I would have dreamed a bigger dream for myself but I didn't know any bigger dreams to dream at that point. The options for the boys after high school were working at the mill or going into military service. Daddy thought that I might get a job as a secretary or a nurse but neither of those jobs sounded very interesting to me.

I didn't know anybody who had gone to college or anybody who was in college so I didn't have a way of imagining what college might be like. I knew that I didn't have the grades or the necessary courses for going to college, and I definitely knew that I didn't have the money for college.

That doesn't mean that I hadn't *heard* about college or that I hadn't been encouraged to consider college. Many of my friends in high school were going to college and they encouraged me to go, too. One of my friends, Tammy, asked me one day, "Eva, what are you going to do next year if you don't go to college?" I said, "I'll work in the mill, get married, and have babies." That was just as foreign an idea to her as college was to me.

Tammy responded to me, "Eva, you can't do that. You could be a teacher." I thought about that . . . but I had no idea what a person had to do to become a teacher.

One of my classes in high school was a class in which I

taught the ninth-grade choir. I did this even though I couldn't read music. I could hear a song and repeat it—on pitch, with all the words, and with the right melody and rhythm—and somehow I managed to teach the choir class with only that amount of skill. The teacher who supervised my conducting the choir said to me one day, "Eva, do you realize that if you told those kids in that choir to go out and jump over that porch rail, they'd do it?"

I said, "Now why would I tell them to jump over that rail?"

He said, "Eva, I'm telling you that you have the power to lead people and that you are capable of influencing young lives. You shouldn't let that go to waste. You are getting ready to graduate and I want you to pray about what you are going to do. If you want to go to college, Eva, there's money to be found."

I heard what he said, but on the other hand, I didn't really hear him. I couldn't see how his words could make any difference in my life after high school. Nobody in my family had gone to college. Nobody in my neighborhood was going to college. College was just out of the question as far as I was concerned. Getting a job, getting married, and having babies were the only dreams I could imagine dreaming.

Mama didn't say anything to discourage me, but I noticed that she was always a little sad when I told her about my plans.

And then I met Alan at a practice for the countywide ensemble. Alan was tall and blond and a great bass singer. In lots of ways, Alan was like a dream. His father played baseball with Daddy so he was accepted by my family. He planned to go to college. He showed an interest in me.

We spent quite a bit of time talking and Alan also

encouraged me to expand my horizons and go to college and get out of Concord. I decided that maybe I didn't want to marry my old boyfriend after all, or have babies by the time I was twenty. So on Valentine's Day of my senior year, I told my boyfriend of three years that I wanted to break up.

Mama's bedroom was right behind the living room where my boyfriend and I were talking so she heard the whole conversation. She heard my boyfriend start to cry, and then get up and run out of the house. I started after him, but before I got to the door, Mama came out of her bedroom and grabbed me from behind. She put her hand on the front door and said, "Don't go after him, Eva. Don't go after him."

She wanted more for me than I wanted for myself. She always did. She saw potential in me, and dreamed dreams for me, even when I didn't.

The Lord dreams big dreams for us. I'm convinced of that. Most of the time His dreams are bigger than the dreams we dream. He sees more in us than we see in ourselves. He really does have a future and a hope for us as the prophet Jeremiah said.

But sometimes getting to the place where we begin to see what God sees isn't easy.

6

The Accident

For the things which are seen are temporary,
but the things which are not seen are eternal.
(2 Corinthians 4:18)

$\mathcal{A}$ little over two months before my high school graduation, my dreams turned to dust.

I was sick that day with a bad cold. I shouldn't even have gone to school that morning, but I did. Later in the day, I went home and laid down because I felt so sick. Daddy didn't want to see me go out again after school because he thought I was too sick to be out. I told him I had drama practice—which was true—but I didn't go to drama practice that day. I drove over to Alan's school to drive him to his house.

After dropping Alan off, I was in a hurry to get home to change clothes before I went to my job at Zayre's Department Store. I had been promoted from a store cashier to the hardware department where I got to help put together lawn mowers. I hardly ever missed work. I loved my job there.

That early March evening as I left Alan's house, the snow started to fall and the temperature began to drop really fast. The roads were icy.

I was driving on a two-lane country road that I knew well. As I came around a turn, a car began to pass two other cars and it headed straight toward me in my lane. I started pumping the brakes so I wouldn't hit that car head-on. The car barely squeezed through the gap between me and the cars it was passing. In hitting the brakes, I caused my car to start fishtailing on the ice. I never did regain control of it.

I was headed straight for the bridge and when I saw that, I hit the brakes as hard as I could to keep from going over it. That sent the car into a spin and the rear end of my

1974 Maverick hit the guard rails with such force that my car flipped over and rolled down the embankment. The rear end of the car ended up in a shallow creek about forty feet below the bridge.

I was conscious the whole time. All of the sounds of the accident—breaking glass, screeching tires—sounded like a slow-motion movie sound track to me. It was almost as if this were happening to someone else, not me. As the car rolled down the hill, I was thrown from the front seat to the backseat several times. When the car finally stopped moving, I found myself on the backseat floorboard. I could hear the radio playing faintly and the windshield wipers still going back and forth. Everything else was still.

A towel that had been over the front seat had flipped into the back with me and it covered the lower part of my body. I looked and saw my leg on the backseat even though I was on the floorboard. My first thought was, *My leg shouldn't be there.* It seemed that it should be closer to my body. I reached up and started hitting my leg and I couldn't feel a thing. I saw blood all over the interior roof of the car and I thought, *My leg has been cut off! It's not connected to me! Please Lord, don't let my leg be cut off. Please Lord, please Lord.* I reached down and pulled up the towel and I saw that my leg was connected to my body, so I immediately thought, *I'm okay. My leg is attached. I'll be all right.*

The back end of the car was completely smashed in and the back windshield was gone. I thought, *My daddy's gonna kill me.* And then I thought, *I'd better get moving. I'm late for work. I've got to get this figured out.* I could see up through the windshield that the bridge was a long way above me.

I tried to sit up and when I did, I felt the worst pain I've ever felt in my life. If my spinal cord wasn't completely severed before that, it was then. I fell back down onto the floorboard and began to look around.

I was able to reach around the front seat to open the driver's-side door. I stuck my head out the door but the door came crashing back down on my head. I couldn't move my head from that point on. The snow was falling on my face. It was my first day of wearing contact lenses and I couldn't move my head so it was a struggle to keep my eyes open with the snow falling directly into my eyes. The pain was horrible but the snow seemed worse.

The cars that saw me fishtailing down the road must have seen me go over the bridge and I'm grateful they did because if the people in those cars hadn't stopped to help me, nobody would have known I was down in that creek bed in a smashed car. I didn't know in those first few minutes after the crash, however, that cars had stopped. All I knew was that I needed help.

I finally cleared my throat and said in a quivering voice, "Umm, help? Help? Is anybody there? Help?" It seems normal in movies or books for people to call for help, but I felt silly and self-conscious and wasn't sure exactly what to say or how loud to yell. Then I heard a woman's voice call back, "Are you all right?"

I knew I wasn't all right but mostly I didn't want to be alone. I said, "Could you come down here please?"

She said, "I can't get to you right now. Don't move your head. Don't move your neck."

I said, "I've already moved my head and my neck."

She said, "Well, don't move them anymore."

I said, "Okay."

She said, "We've called for help to come. Where were you going?"

I said, "I was going home."

She said, "Are you all right? Can you move your arms? Can you move your legs?"

I said, "I don't have any feeling in my legs." At that, the woman screamed. Up to that point I wasn't scared but after she screamed, I began to feel afraid. I said, "I'd feel a lot better if you all could come here. If you came down here, I'd feel a lot better. I'm cold. Can somebody come down here?"

I heard sirens come to the bridge and then I heard somebody splashing through the creek. The rescue workers were cutting through the door to get to me and most of this time, I was conscious but I kept my eyes shut, trying not to feel cold and trying not to feel scared.

When I opened my eyes, I saw Sam, an old family friend, leaning over me. He was part of the rescue team and I said, "Sam, how are you doing?"

He said, "I'm okay. How are *you* doing?" I could tell he didn't know who I was, probably from all the blood everywhere. I said, "Sam, it's me, Eva." It was obvious that he hadn't recognized me. I said, "Sam, am I going to get the feeling back in my legs?"

Sam ignored my question. He said, "Eva, you have a really bad cut on your head. That's where all this blood is coming from."

Sam got me on a back board and then I heard him calling for more help. I could hear several guys splashing through the creek, saying, "Whooeee," and "Wow, that's cold!"

Sam was tending to me and when the ambulance doors shot open at the hospital, Sam was helping me out of the ambulance and I felt really scared. I grabbed Sam by his lapels and pulled his face close to mine and said, "Sam, am

I ever going to feel my legs again?" He looked me right in the eyes and said, "I don't know, Eva." I was terrified by his answer.

I looked around the hospital as they wheeled me in and there was Daddy looking mad, and Mama in tears, and one of my brothers, his wife, and their daughter. I thought, *Oh no, why are they all here?* I was still thinking that whatever was wrong with me could be fixed pretty quickly and I still had a chance to make it to work, although I might be a little late. I thought once the doctors had caused the feeling to come back in my legs, I'd be able to walk over to a pay phone and call for a ride. I had no idea how serious my situation was.

In the emergency room, one of the nurses took a device and ripped the sides of my clothes and stripped them from my body. I was wearing jeans, a blue cotton button-down, and a blue cardigan. I had purchased those clothes with money I had earned, so I wasn't too happy they had sliced away my clothes—and especially my favorite sweater from the mall in Charlotte! It was humiliating to lie there with a hospital gown on top of me.

Mama came into my room first and sat with me for a while. Then she left and Daddy came in. He said, "Eva, I told you what too much of something would do to you." He was referring to the fact that he had warned me not to go out when I was sick, and especially not to go to Alan's house. Daddy had really liked my former boyfriend and he thought Alan liked me only because I had a car and would drive him anywhere he wanted to go at the drop of a hat.

I said, "Daddy, I'm probably going to die today. And after I do, I want you to know that you were right and I was wrong, and I hope that makes you feel good." I didn't look at him while I spoke but I was angry at him. I certainly didn't *really* think I was dying. I just wanted a little more kindness and a little less anger while I was lying there in pain.

Daddy often said things he didn't mean. Many times when I was growing up, Daddy would say something that didn't make sense to my brother or me and we always turned to Mama to interpret for us. She'd say, "What your daddy really meant was . . ." It was classic alcoholic behavior but I didn't know that at the time.

In that moment, Daddy didn't know how to respond to a situation in which his daughter was badly injured. When Daddy got into situations that he couldn't control or that were painful for him, he got angry. When Mama felt pain, she cried and prayed. Neither anger nor tears helped very much in that moment, but I'm sure the prayer helped.

Mama wasn't the only one praying. The news of my accident spread quickly. My friends and their family members from school gathered that night to pray for me.

My best friend at school was Bobby Dale and as soon as he heard about the accident, he came to the hospital. Bobby Dale and I loved watching the *Gong Show* together, and he showed up as they wheeled me out for X rays. He started acting out Gong Show routines to make me laugh—dancing all around the room and acting silly as he tried to cheer me up. But he had tears running down his face while he was dancing. Neither of us felt much like laughing. Bobby Dale told me later that he was afraid I was going to die that night. I sensed that fear in him and it was at that point that I began to wonder if I really *was* going to die.

The doctors knew immediately that I was paralyzed and they told my family I was paralyzed. Nobody told me, however. The doctors decided that I needed to be transported to the larger hospital in Charlotte, so I was loaded up again into an ambulance and we made our way on the icy roads to Charlotte about forty-five minutes away.

The intensive care unit was my home for the next week as the doctors tried to stabilize me for surgery.

Even though I was in intensive care, I had visitors almost constantly. The day after the accident was a snow day at school. Even so, my friends Ashlyn, Alan, and Bobby Dale braved the snow and ignored the "Family Only" signs in the intensive care unit and they came to my room, and so did one of my teachers.

Everyone kept telling me those first few days in the hospital how proud they were of me and how brave I was. When night came and I was all alone in the darkness of the intensive care unit, I was anything but brave.

I'd lie awake staring at the ceiling and listening to the moans and screams of other patients and the footsteps of nurses rushing to bedsides. When I did sleep, I had terrible nightmares about monsters or endless falling—the kind of dreams in which you try to cry for help but you can't make a sound.

I got a stack of cards every day—I remember opening some of them and watching the nurses tape them on the walls all around the bed so I could see them. But other than the moments with my visitors and the cards, I remember very little about the days in intensive care. Those first days in the hospital were a blur—of people, of cards, of bad dreams, of staring blankly at the ceiling. I was on pain medication and was mostly out of it. I'm grateful for that—there wasn't a lot of time to think.

People have asked me, "Eva, did you blame God?"

No. I was too hurt at that time to even think about "why" the accident happened. The snow . . . the passing cars . . . the ice on the road . . . those were the things that "caused" my accident.

People have also asked, "Eva, *do* you blame God?"

The answer to that question—one that I've faced many times over twenty years—is also no.

God is sovereign. I don't know all the reasons *why* I had the accident, but I know that God knows all the reasons. In many ways, that accident was the best thing that ever happened to me. On the surface, it is the worst thing that has happened to me in my life. But when it comes to things that are eternal and really meaningful, it was the best thing.

There are those who say that God didn't cause the accident. Others say that He did. All I know is that it was the most difficult experience of my life and I'd never want to go through it again, but if that's what it took for me to know the Lord—really *know* Him—then I'd do it again because nothing can ever matter as much as knowing Him.

I once had a man ask me, "What is a soul worth? Is it worth a dime? Is it worth five dollars? Is it worth an arm? Is it worth two legs?"

At the time I said to him, "Hey, how about your two legs instead of mine?" But the truth is— there is no price that can be put on a soul. If the price for me was losing the use of my legs, that price is nothing compared to what I have gained for all eternity.

Now I didn't learn all that right away. Those lessons and conclusions came little by little, piece by piece. My recovery from the accident was not fast. But God was faithful and patient. He always is.

7

"Why, God, Why?"

"For My thoughts are not your thoughts,
Nor are your ways My ways," says the LORD.
"For as the heavens are higher than the earth,
So are My ways higher than your ways,
And My thoughts than your thoughts."
(Isaiah 55:8–9)

*A*lthough I never blamed God for my accident, I can't say that I never questioned Him about it. For the first ten days in intensive care, nothing was really done about my back. Before they could schedule surgery, the doctors first had to deal with my bad cold and the very real possibility of pneumonia.

As a result of this delay, I didn't learn the extent or the precise nature of my injuries until a week and a half after the accident. My doctor walked into my room and began to tell me about the procedure that he was going to perform on my back and how he was going to fuse the bones of my spine back together.

The doctor explained that my spinal cord was completely severed at the L-1 level, very low on my back. The surgery would involve a fusion of the first two lumbar vertebrae. They would also have to put in two steel Harrington rods to stabilize my spine so I could sit in an upright position.

After he had told me what was going to happen during the surgery, he asked me if I had any questions. I had dozens of questions, so many that I hardly knew which one to ask first. I finally decided on the most important question that I needed to ask as a seventeen-year-old girl, and after he answered me, I didn't need to ask any other questions. I asked the doctor, "When will I be able to walk again?"

He looked at me and said, "Never, Eva. You'll never ever walk again." And he walked out of the room.

After he had gone, I screamed as loud as I could, "Why, God, why? What have I done that was so terrible that I deserve this?"

I don't know about you, but when something bad happens to me, I can tell you every good thing I've ever done since birth as a reason why this bad thing shouldn't be happening to *me*. The fact was, I was a good girl!

I went to church every Sunday.

I said my prayers every night.

Not once in my life had I ever smoked a cigarette or had a drink. The strongest alcoholic beverage I have ever tasted is a spoonful of cough medicine! I was a virgin.

I had been taught all my life to be a "good girl." And every day, I tried to be good. I'd say to myself in the mornings as I got ready for school, "I'm going to be a good girl all day long." I never did make it through a whole day as a good girl—somewhere along the line I'd lose my temper or have bad thoughts about somebody or use a swear word or tell a little lie. But my failures didn't keep me from trying every morning to be good all day the *next* day. I knew being a good girl was important and I wanted to be a good girl.

I had the idea that God did good things for good girls. Bad things just didn't happen to really good girls. So, the only reason I could see for the accident was that I must not have been good.

I lay there in my self-righteousness. And of course, you know what the Scriptures say about our self-righteousness—"all our righteousnesses are like filthy rags" (Isa. 64:6). I lay there in my filthy rags trying to figure out "why."

Nothing could have been farther from the truth, of course, than the idea that my "goodness" or "badness" was somehow related to the accident. In the first place, I wasn't "good" because I did certain things and didn't do other things. Any goodness that we have before God is solely because of what Jesus has done for us and in us. In the second place, bad things *do* happen to good people. In the third place—and most important of all—God is with us even when bad things happen. He showed me how He could bring good out of bad, and make Himself real to me in the midst of it all.

God can never be reduced to a formula. He can't be put in a box. He is bigger than all our ideas about Him. When I read the Bible, I see that God healed people in different ways. Sometimes Jesus touched people . . . sometimes He spoke to people . . . and once He spit on the clay and then put that wet clay on a man's eyes and he was healed. In my old way of thinking, I would have been quick to say, "Well, I'll be one of the Spit-ites and God will heal me *that* way." But God doesn't do things our way. He does things *His* way.

God, and only God, can take awful things, broken things, things that are in a million pieces, and make them and shape them and mold them for His purposes and for our good.

The Lord is still teaching me those lessons. Right at that moment, however, I only knew that God had somehow blown up all my ideas about good and bad behavior. He was about to start teaching me about mercy and grace.

8

$\mathcal{A}$ Visit from Mr. Ed

*Rejoice with those who rejoice, and
weep with those who weep.
(Romans 12:15)*

'm so glad that God gave me full permission to tell Him exactly how I felt at that time. I'm grateful that we can question God. It's at the point where we empty our hearts out to God that He can begin to fill us with Himself. It's at the point where we begin to question that God can start giving us His answers.

I certainly was in a position for *receiving* answers. Actually, I was in a position for receiving just about everything at that time. There was very little I could do for myself.

For nine weeks after my accident, both before and after the surgery, I lived on a Stryker frame. The purpose of the Stryker frame was to keep my back straight and to keep me from getting pressure sores.

A Stryker frame looks like a flat cot about two or three feet above the floor. It was so narrow that if I put my hands down by my sides, they would both fall straight to the floor.

Every two hours, the nurses would bring in another frame almost exactly like the one on which I was lying. The only difference was that this piece had straps to secure my forehead and my chin. The nurses would lay that second frame on top of me and secure both frames with belts tied around them, with me in the middle. Then they would count, "One, two, three" and on three, they'd flip me over so I was facing the floor. Then the belts were removed and the top piece was removed. This procedure was repeated every two hours, day and night, for nine weeks.

After I had screamed at God and had become quiet

again, the nurses came into my room because it was time to flip me over onto my stomach. They left again after they had turned the Stryker frame and I lay there staring down at the floor. I was crying when they came into my room and I was crying when they left. Crying was all I could do.

Up to the time the doctor told me that I'd never walk again, I had the idea that when the doctors finally did my surgery, they'd fix my legs and I'd have feeling again and be back to normal. Most of my friends at school thought the same thing.

I had phantom leg pains and my friends interpreted the pain as my having "feeling" in my leg. Everybody was very optimistic that I was going to have a full recovery. I was optimistic, too.

All of that optimism came crashing down around me when the doctor said I'd never walk again.

The nurses must have thought it was best to leave me alone to sort through my feelings and my pain because nobody came into my room for quite a while after I had been turned. God knew that what I really needed was not a nurse, anyway, but rather a visit from my pastor friend, Mr. Ed.

Mr. Ed was what I called him. His name was really Ed Hall and he was the pastor of the Pitts Baptist Church in Concord. His son, Jimmy, was in the ninth-grade choir that I helped direct.

Mr. Ed walked into my room and said cheerfully, "Hey, Eva, it's Mr. Ed. How are you doing?" Then he noticed that I was crying and he asked me what was wrong. I told him what the doctor had just said—that I would never walk again.

Mr. Ed was a big man. He had a suit on that day. I don't know what I expected him to do, but I sure didn't expect him to do what he did. In the midst of my despair and grief, that big man walked over to me, got down on the floor, lay down on his back, and positioned himself so I could see his face and he could see mine. He reached up and took my hand and he cried with me.

He didn't say a thing. He didn't try to cheer me up or give me false hope by telling me that I'd walk again. He didn't preach a sermon to me, he didn't give me any theology or quote the Bible to me . . . he just hurt with me. After he had cried with me for quite some time, he prayed for me and he told me that lots of people were praying for me and that God had a special purpose for my life. By the time he left, I had stopped crying and he was still crying.

The Lord knew I needed a friend like that—someone who could cry with me when crying was the only thing that made any sense.

Through the years, I have been nervous at times when I have gone to funeral homes or when I have met people who have had a tragedy in their lives. I didn't know what to say. I finally realized that I don't need to say anything. I just need to be like Mr. Ed. Just being there, just giving a little hug or saying "I love you" is enough. Proverbs 10:19 says, "In the multitude of words sin is not lacking, but he who restrains his lips is wise." I believe there's a great lesson in that verse that most of us still need to learn.

God met me where I was that day, and He met me through Mr. Ed. I didn't have a great spiritual experience or even feel all that much better after I had cried and screamed at God. But God met me and I eventually calmed down. Mr. Ed happened to come in right at the moment when I needed someone like him the most. I don't have any doubt that God sent him.

I don't know who God will send to you when you need someone the most. But I believe He'll send the right person to you at exactly the right time. What He did for me, He'll do for you.

9

A Roller Coaster of Highs and Lows

The LORD has anointed Me . . .
To comfort all who mourn, . . .
To give them beauty for ashes,
The oil of joy for mourning,
The garment of praise for the spirit of heaviness;
That they may be called trees of righteousness,
The planting of the LORD, that He may be glorified.
(Isaiah 61:1–3)

$\mathcal{T}$he Charlotte Rehabilitation Hospital was my home for three months. It was an old building with peeling plaster on the walls and green tile floors. I had big windows in my room and I remember the first time I was rolled into the room and the curtains were opened. It was spring! The trees were covered with little green leaves and the sky was blue and it looked warm. It was the first time I had seen the outside world in three weeks.

It's amazing to me how what we see affects our attitudes. When I was in the Stryker frame, the view of the world I had when I was on my stomach was pretty much limited to the floor. I had to eat and brush my teeth in that position since I couldn't do either when I was flat on my back. Sometimes the nurses would get busy and leave my food tray or the rinse water from my tooth brushing on the floor directly under my face. I still don't like to look in the sink when I'm brushing my teeth.

Although I finally was in a room with windows, my days in rehabilitation were anything but "sunny all the way." Instead, they were something of an emotional roller coaster. I struggled every day with the *idea* of my paralysis, even as I went to a round of physical therapy sessions.

In the first month or so after my accident, eight well-meaning people gave me a copy of Joni Eareckson's book on her experience with paralysis. I know now that they were trying to help me, and that their efforts were to give me hope in the midst of my struggle. I could tell they were comparing me to Joni and hoping somehow to lessen the blow of my becoming a paraplegic. After all, Joni was a quadriplegic. I was irritated, however, that these people were so cheerful as they gave me her book.

It took me several weeks before I finally picked up one of those books and started to read it. While I was reading, Dr. Dewberry came into my room to tell me that they were going to try a new type of back brace on me—instead of a body cast—to prepare me for the next phase of my rehabilitation. And then he dropped a bombshell. He told me that the brace would not be ready in time for me to go to my high school graduation. I hate to admit it—I threw Joni Eareckson's inspirational book, in hard cover, directly at him and only narrowly missed!

I'll never forget the day when my physical therapists and I were talking while they were doing range-of-motion exercises with my legs. I was telling the therapists about being a cheerleader and a basketball player and I complained about having such big calves from all those years of athletic activity and bike riding.

At that very moment, one of the therapists raised my leg high enough that I could see it. I couldn't believe she was holding my leg. It was so small! I thought, *That can't be my leg.* My legs' muscles had atrophied so fast! When she brought my leg up for the second time, I reached up and grabbed my calf and began to cry.

I thought a number of times in the hospital, *I really* am *dying. Nobody has the nerve to tell me, but I'm dying.* I didn't know anything about muscle atrophy and when I saw my leg so thin and realized I was losing a great deal of weight, I concluded I was slowly dying.

In some ways, I believe I really was dying in that hospital —spiritually. I was dying to my old ideas about God. I was dying to my old identity as Eva the Athlete, Eva the

Cheerleader, Eva the Girlfriend, Eva the Popular Friend. Charles Spurgeon once said, "When you get to the end of yourself, you get to the beginning of God." The old Eva was getting to the end of herself.

When you get to the place where the Lord is all you have, you really are in the best position to discover that He is all you need.

Nights were the worst times for me.

Many nights I stared at the ceiling in the hospital and told God how scared I was. I was afraid that no one would really, truly love me in a wheelchair. I was afraid of seeing pity in people's eyes. I was desperately afraid of losing Alan. I'd close my eyes and pretend that it was all a nightmare and that I'd never been in an accident, I wasn't really paralyzed, and I'd soon wake up and discover that I was back to my normal self. Then the squeaky wheel of a nurse's cart or the beep of a monitor would jar me back to reality.

I called Daddy one weekend night from the hospital and awoke him. I told him how lonely I was and that I just needed to talk. He didn't know what to say since I usually talked to Mama, and he started crying with me on the phone.

The next day, I heard Daddy coming down the hall. He wore heel taps on his shoes and when he walked, he made a distinctive clicking sound on the tile floors. I could always hear him coming. He came into my room and with a sheepish look on his face, he held out my favorite doll, Susie. A woman had given Susie to Mama for me on the day I was born and she represented everything that was good and happy about my childhood. As Daddy handed this old plastic, beat-up doll to me, he said, "Maybe this will help you sleep better, honey. She's always been there for you."

Susie was of greater *comfort* to me than Joni Eareckson's

book because she was a tie to the happy days of my past. She wasn't necessarily a greater *help*.

One of the worst physical side effects of the paralysis has been what is commonly called "phantom pains." In phantom pains, a burning begins in my heels and begins tingling up my calves to the top of my legs and then a sharp searing pain shoots back down my legs.

It seems to me that paraplegics who have lots of leg spasms have very few phantom pains, and those who have phantom pains don't have many spasms. I've never had leg spasms, but I have had phantom pains almost daily since the accident. The pain is nearly always present, but sometimes it's more intense than at other times.

At the beginning, I got such intense leg pains that there were a few times when I actually prayed for God to let me die because I didn't think I could endure the intensity of pain any longer. When I asked Dr. Dewberry if this terrible pain would eventually stop, or if I could get some medicine for it, he told me that I would have phantom pains for the rest of my life and that I would have to learn to live with them because the painkillers I needed were too addictive. The only permanent medical solution would be to clip the nerves into my legs, and that "solution" has its own side effects. I finally did get some medicine that helped, but in the end, it has been exactly as Dr. Dewberry said—I have had to learn to live with pain. As a seventeen-year-old, however, living with pain did not seem like a very good life.

Not all of my rehabilitation experience was grim and dire. Life is never a hundred percent one way or the other. There were lighthearted moments—like the time I tipped over in a wheelchair in the rose garden, where I wasn't supposed to be, and nearly missed physical therapy as a result.

There were races with other wheelchair patients through the underground tunnel to get to the cafeteria that had the best food. And there were strangers who seemed to come out of nowhere to show incredible kindness.

I especially remember the kindness of one particular nurse on prom night.

Before the accident, I had really been looking forward to my senior prom. My former boyfriend had never wanted to go to a school prom with me but *this* year, I figured I'd not only get to go to my prom but I'd also get to go with Alan to the prom at his school. I was going to make up for lost time!

I had a hard time as prom night came closer and I realized that I wasn't going to get to go to any prom. I had secretly hoped that I'd be in a wheelchair by prom time and that I'd be able to make a grand entrance in a beautiful long dress. Even though I knew I couldn't dance, I figured at least I'd be there and look beautiful. When prom time came, however, I was still on the Stryker frame.

Several of my friends came by the hospital to visit me on prom night. They had come from Concord to Charlotte for dinner at a fancy restaurant before the prom, so they stopped by in their tuxedos and new dresses so I could see them and be as much a part of the event as possible. Alan came by with my friend Ashlyn and I was happy they both could go to the prom. The smells of their colognes and corsages filled my room and after they left, a tremendous sadness settled in.

I think that was the beginning of my facing the fact that life wasn't going to turn out exactly as I had planned . . . or dreamed . . . or hoped. Eva wasn't going to get to do all the things she wanted to do—at least not when she wanted to do them.

Reality is a hard lesson. God knows that, I think. Even as

He allows us to confront the truth about our lives and about situations that we face, He also sends someone to comfort us.

One of the fun-loving, younger nurses sensed that I was sad. She came to my room after her shift was over and she brought with her a huge box of assorted chocolates. We ate chocolates and traded stories until late into the night.

She didn't have to do that. It was a great example of kindness to me.

Another person who came to mean a great deal to me was a stranger named Bill, a truck driver in Concord, who heard about me at his church and stopped by to visit me "out of the blue." After that first visit, he stopped by frequently, whenever he wasn't driving the truck, just to talk. We became good friends.

One day I shared with Bill my concern about my phone bill and the other bills that still had to be paid. The insurance I had through Mama's employment covered a good portion of my doctor and hospital bills, but there were a number of things that weren't covered, such as my back brace . . . and my phone bill. The calls home to family and friends were long-distance calls, which meant that I had a very large phone bill in a very short period of time!

A while after that conversation, Bill came into my room all smiles and said, "I just heard some good news, Eva. I heard that your phone bill has been paid."

"Who did that?" I asked. He said, "Well, I hear angels do things like that sometimes." I knew Bill was the angel in this case although he never would admit it.

I tried to keep the kindness of people like Bill in mind when I went to physical therapy. And especially as I faced the tilt table.

After a person has been horizontal on a Stryker frame

for as long as I had been, the next step is the tilt table. The tilt table is a big rectangular "card table." The purpose of the tilt table was to help me transition from the prone position of the Stryker frame to an upright position. Each day I lay on the tilt table and it was raised an inch or two at a time, with the goal being that the tilt table would eventually be in an upright position—a position that usually takes weeks to be reached.

The frustrating thing about this process was not knowing *exactly* how long it would take to get to that upright position. I had no control over how my body would respond on any given day to a given degree of "tilt." When I was finally brought to a full standing position on the table and my feet didn't turn purple and I didn't throw up or pass out, then I could begin to use a wheelchair.

One day when I was on the tilt table, I was feeling sorry for myself because I was having a hard time and I kept getting sick. As I began to cry, I saw a group of children coming down the hall outside the therapy room—they were on their way to the cafeteria. Most of them were between five and ten years old. Some of the kids were in wheelchairs, one little boy was in a boxlike contraption with only his arms sticking out, and some used walkers, were on crutches, or in leg braces. They were typical children in every other way—rowdy, noisy, and rambunctious.

Once these kids got to the cafeteria, they began to sing a song as their teacher played the piano. The words were:

> If I were a crocodile, I'd thank the Lord for making me smile.
> And if I were a fuzzy bear, I'd thank Him for my fuzzy, wuzzy hair.

I just thank You, Father for making me me,
'Cause You gave me a heart, You gave me a smile,
You gave me Jesus and You made me Your child.
And I just thank You, Father, for making me me.

I could understand every word of their song as they all joined in. I felt as if the Lord were speaking directly to me. Here were all these little crippled boys and girls singing a song about being thankful that God had made them just the way they were. I felt humbled before the Lord.

I realized that some of these children had never walked or run as I had as a child, and that none of them were ever going to play basketball or be a cheerleader. These boys and girls had never felt sand between their toes, played football in their backyard, or chased a puppy. I began to cry for them. And I began to thank the Lord for the experiences He had allowed me to have.

It's so much easier to count our problems instead of our blessings. Sometimes we just have to *make* ourselves thank God for the good things He gives us and to praise Him for who He is.

Something good happens inside us, however, when we choose to be thankful to the Lord *in the midst of our circumstances*. Something good happens when we start praising God even while we are experiencing pain or are struggling. That's the start of a healing on the inside, even though nothing on the outside may seem very different.

I had gone from having a false hope, to having no hope, to having *real* hope. That final turnaround came when I began to praise and give thanks *even in the midst* of my circumstances.

10

raduation Days

Through the Lord's mercies we are not consumed,
Because His compassions fail not.
They are new every morning;
Great is Your faithfulness.
(Lamentations 3:22–23)

ortunately, the brace that I had been told wouldn't be available in time for my high school graduation did come in time. It allowed me to move from the tilt table to a special type of wheelchair, not at all like the one I use today.

This wheelchair was constructed so the nurses could check for pressure sores and it was mostly a chair in which I was to *sit*. Every day, the physical therapists would recline the back and raise the foot rests when they transferred me into the chair. And then they would lift the back of the chair a few degrees and lower my feet a few degrees. This transition took several weeks. It was only after I was able to sit for thirty minutes without feeling pain or nausea from the sitting that I was expected to make a wheelchair move.

I was excited the day I finally "graduated" to a normal wheelchair. The goal they gave me was to push myself from my room to the gym, which was only about a hundred feet down the hall.

No problem! I thought. I pushed those wheels a few inches and I couldn't believe how hard it was. I felt as if I were trying to push a thousand pounds. The nurses and aides all knew they weren't to help me, so I really was on my own. I'd push a few feet, then stop and rest, then push a few feet, and stop and rest. And along the way, I cried. My arm muscles were so weak I couldn't push the wheels of the chair around more than once or twice. My tears were tears of frustration, humiliation, and anger. I even felt anger at the doctors and nurses who walked past me, totally ignoring me—all for my own good, but it didn't *feel* that way at the time. It took me almost thirty minutes to roll that first one hundred feet as an independent, wheelchair-bound paraplegic.

There were other humbling moments. One of the therapists began to work with me on balance. I was transferred to a sitting position on a table and all the therapist wanted me to do was to put my hands in front of me and then move them straight out to my side. I had no balance and I flopped all over the place. People don't realize how much their legs balance their upper body motion, and in not having the feeling in my legs, I had to learn a whole new system of balance. It's a little like learning how to walk on stilts, except that there are no stilts.

I began to work on pulleys to get more strength in my arms and upper body. Various therapists came in to try to help me learn how to dress myself and take care of myself. One of the therapists one day helped me into a pair of pants and I didn't realize until later that she had not put any underwear on me first. I was very upset. She said, "What's the matter? You can't feel anyway." I said, "I know I can't feel but I *know*."

I made good progress and before long, I was able to wheel with several of the other patients through the underground tunnel over to the regular hospital to eat in that cafeteria rather than the cafeteria in the rehab center.

I was allowed to check out of the rehabilitation hospital for the day of my high school graduation. My friend Blumers—her real name was Kim Blume—picked me up on graduation morning in her green convertible Mustang. Blumers was a free spirit and as we careened through the busy, downtown Charlotte traffic, I held on for dear life. It was only the second time I'd been in a car since my accident. All of the other cars and trucks seemed very close to us—

too close—and I was just sure I was going to be thrown out of the passenger seat because I felt so off-balance.

When we were stopped at a stoplight, I said to her, "Blumers, don't we seem close to these other vehicles?"

She put her hand out and touched the 18-wheeler next to us and said, "You're right, Eva! We sure are close!"

The graduation ceremony was held in the gym because it was raining so hard that the program couldn't be held on the football field as usual. I had butterflies in my stomach while I was waiting for the processional. Since I was a "W," I had to wait for most of the alphabet to march in and take their seats before I was rolled in. It seemed to take forever. A sophomore named Tommy had been chosen to be my escort for the ceremony. He was sweet and kept telling me that I looked nice and that it was an honor for him to escort me. When my name was called and I was lifted in my wheelchair onto the platform, the people in the audience started to clap for me and within seconds, they were giving me a standing ovation. I was happy and honored, but also embarrassed—especially since the audience had been asked to hold their applause until all of the seniors received their diplomas. Tommy, however, was excited about all the applause and he stood there on the stage grinning for several more moments before he finally wheeled me off!

After the ceremony, parents and graduates were invited to the gym lobby for a reception and I heard lots of them talking about their plans to go to Charlotte for dinner celebrations. I, however, had to return to the hospital with Mama and Daddy. I couldn't join my friends for the rest of the fun and the unfairness of my situation really hit me hard that night. Graduation was the night I had always seen as the climax of my entire life!

At this point, I really started to crave freedom. If I couldn't get out of my wheelchair, at least I could get out of the hospital. If I couldn't graduate from high school in the style I wanted, at least I could graduate from rehab.

One of the final steps of my rehabilitation was learning how to drive a car with hand controls. The hand controls were connected by steel rods to the gas and brake pedals. If I pulled back on the handle, the car went forward. If I pushed the handle rod, the car would stop. And in the meantime, I had to steer while manipulating the levers. I was confident that I could master the hand controls quickly.

I dreamed about picking up friends for a trip to the mall or cruising through a fast-food drive-through. I figured no one would be able to tell I was crippled when I was sitting behind the wheel of a car.

The second time I went out with the driving instructor, he directed me to drive into downtown Charlotte. I had never driven in downtown Charlotte traffic *before* my accident, much less with hand controls.

I approached one stoplight as it changed to red and I immediately began to try to put on the brakes with my foot. My foot, of course, didn't move, but my upper body was in the position for a screeching halt. The car, however, didn't slow down in the least. Finally, the instructor took over the controls and we stopped . . . barely in time to avoid running the light.

He turned to me and calmly said, "Eva, now that we're paralyzed, how do we put on the brakes?" *We?* I thought. *I'm the one who's paralyzed with fear right now. What do you mean, how do we put on the brakes?* I didn't say anything, however. I just pointed to the hand control and said, "With this thing right here." He immediately said, "I think you're ready for the driving test." And we drove over to the Department of Motor Vehicles and I passed on the first try. I was eager to be in control of a car again. It was a big sign of freedom to me.

I felt ready to go *home*.

11

Home Again

Seek first the kingdom of God and His righteousness,
and all these things shall be added to you.
(Matthew 6:33)

*O*nce I was able to transfer into and out of my wheelchair, wheel myself around, and had learned to drive, dress myself, and catheterize myself, I had done just about everything the hospital was prepared to help me do.

The nurses and physical therapists all reported in my exit interviews that I had done amazingly well in my physical rehabilitation. My athletic ability and competitive drive had paid off.

I also had completed the number of prescribed "home visits." Before I could be fully discharged from the hospital, I had to spend a prescribed number of weekends at home. On those weekends, Mama and Daddy would come and pick me up on Saturday morning and take me back by Saturday night. Then they'd come again on Sunday morning and take me back to the hospital by Sunday night. The weekends at home had gone without a hitch.

I still wasn't ready on the inside, however, to go home. The psychiatrist knew it. I didn't.

We had group therapy sessions on Fridays and I didn't like that part of the rehabilitation at all. I didn't enjoy talking about being a paraplegic or about how I felt about my paralysis. I'd listen to the other people talk and, for the most part, I tried not to say anything.

On one particular day, I became the "topic of discussion" for the group. I resented that. In particular, the group discussed whether I was still in denial. I may have been, but if I was, I didn't want to have everybody discussing my denial!

The psychiatrist that I met with asked me privately, "What are you going to do when you get out of the hospital?" This question was part of the goal-setting process that the hospital felt was important in the recovery of paralyzed patients. I replied to the therapist, "I'll go back to my job at Zayre's Department Store and work my way up to management."

The therapist said, "Well, that's good, but why don't you take the ACT or SAT test just in case you decide you want to go to college?" I said, "I didn't take college prep classes and I'm not smart enough for college and I'm not going to college so why should I take the test?" He said, "Well, you have to take the test before we let you out of the hospital."

I agreed to take the test but I fell asleep during the middle of it. I just wasn't interested. I wanted to go home, continue my relationship with Alan, get my job back, get married, and go on with the old life I had planned.

The psychiatrist finally said to me, "You've said all the right things to me but I think you're still living in a dream world. You're not ready to go home yet." He was right. Still, everything was checked off on paper so I was released.

On the day I was discharged from the hospital, nobody was happier than Daddy. The nurses cried and told me how much they'd miss me and they made me promise to come back and visit. Mama was in tears and I was crying, too. But Daddy was humming and whistling and joking with everyone —his little girl was finally coming home. He wouldn't let anybody else roll me to the car in my brand-new, customized, fluorescent orange wheelchair.

Once I got home, *nothing* was as I had thought it would be. So many people had come to see me in the hospital and at the rehabilitation hospital that my stay there had been something of a nonstop party. I think I figured that when I got home, all my friends would continue to come by and the party would go on.

My friends, however, didn't come as they had in the hospital. I knew that it was difficult for them to see me so thin. I had lost about seventy pounds while I was in the hospital. I thought I looked good—after all, I could finally tuck my shirt into my jeans without looking fat—but to my family and friends, I looked sick. I'm five-foot ten-inches "long," and at the time I went home from the rehabilitation hospital, I weighed only a hundred pounds. When I look back at the pictures now, I think I look anorexic.

Not all of my friends were distant. Tammy spent a lot of time that summer driving me around in her car as we ran errands. The passenger door on Tammy's car didn't open due to a little fender bender, so I'd have to swing out of my wheelchair into the driver's seat and then slide across the seat until I finally plopped into the passenger seat. Tammy would then hoist my wheelchair into the backseat and off we'd go. Most of our errands involved going to visit Alan at his dad's hardware store or visiting Scott, Alan's best friend and the object of a big crush for Tammy.

Then the summer began to fall apart.

Tammy prepared to leave for Western Carolina University. She was planning to be a special education teacher and I thought she'd be a great one. My other friends didn't come around as much. They were busy getting on with their lives, some of them getting jobs and others heading off to college like Tammy. It was a normal transition season in their lives . . . but not in mine. I was stuck in the same place I had been, only in a wheelchair.

To make matters worse, I did *not* get my job back at Zayre's as I had felt so certain I would. There was concern from the insurance people that I'd be further injured on the job. For several weeks, I was at home with nothing to do and nobody to do it with.

I began to cling more and more to Alan, which must have put tremendous pressure on him.

A friend could tell I was feeling depressed and she invited me to go to the beach with her. The night before we left, Alan came over and broke up with me. I was hurt and angry at the same time. I accused him of being cruel in not breaking up with me while I was in the hospital so I could get over it there, and I put a real guilt trip on him about leaving me just because I was paralyzed. What could he say? He said he'd always love me, never leave me, and with that promise that I knew in my heart wasn't a real promise, I went to the beach.

I called Alan repeatedly when I got back from the trip but he didn't answer my calls. When a friend finally answered Alan's phone, I could hear Alan in the background but he didn't want to talk to me. I knew immediately that our relationship was over. I sat in my room wondering what I should do.

About that time, my friend Keith came over for a visit and I asked him to drive me over to Alan's to get my high school ring back. Alan wasn't home so it was a frustrating experience. When we got back home, I said to Keith, "I don't know what I'm going to do. I just don't want to live anymore. I thought my life was set. I was going to marry Alan and go back to my job and get on with my life. Now what?"

Keith said, "Eva, you need to read your Bible."

I said, "Keith, I know what the Bible says. I've been in church all my life. I don't need a sermon right now."

He said, "Eva, just promise me you'll read it for yourself." I promised him . . . but I didn't start reading right away. I still hadn't hit bottom.

As the days dragged on . . . no Alan, no friends, and no job . . . I got to the point where I didn't want to wake up in the mornings. I'd look out my window and see the sun shining, but it didn't matter. I'd look over and see my bright orange wheelchair and think, *That's what crippled people sit in.* I couldn't wait for the sun to go down so I could shut out the world and go to sleep, but most nights, I didn't sleep. I lay awake for hours just staring into the darkness.

Eventually, I was hired back at Zayre's as a part-time cashier on the six to ten shift at night. The store built a little platform so I could reach the cash register in my wheelchair and I was grateful to be back on the job. The work gave me some sense of purpose and people to talk to.

I was still depressed, though, and in those dark days, I even made a couple of feeble, halfhearted attempts at suicide. When I look back on what I did, I don't think I really thought either time that I was putting an end to my life. I was simply looking for a way to deal with the pain I felt—and not waking up seemed like a better idea than waking up.

I believe in the power of prayer and I believe that in those darkest moments of my life—days that were even darker than those immediately following the accident— somebody was praying for me. It probably was Mama, although she never said.

I finally said to the Lord, "Lord, I feel like half a person, but all that I am belongs to You. Will You do something with Eva?" The Lord said back to my heart, *Eva, I want to take you just as you are, and I will make you into the* best *you that you can possibly be.*

I also began to do two things that radically changed my life.

First, I began to pray as I never had before. I'm not talking about saying grace before a meal or saying the Lord's Prayer before bedtime. I'm talking about setting aside a specific time every day to talk with the Lord. I didn't stop talking to the Lord until I knew that He had heard me and I didn't stop listening until I knew that I had heard from Him.

Second, I took the challenge that Keith had given me. I got out the old black Bible I received when I was baptized at the age of eight in the Methodist Church, and I set a goal for myself of reading a chapter a day. I started with Matthew. The first day I read the first chapter of Matthew, and I have to admit, it didn't do a lot for me. It was filled with "So-and-so begat so-and-so, and so-and-so begat so-and-so." But I stuck with my reading and after several days, I was into the Sermon on the Mount. I came across a verse there that I had known all my life. In fact, I had not only read it, but I had sung it, memorized it, and even cross-stitched it and hung it on my wall. It was Matthew 6:33—"Seek first the kingdom of God and His righteousness, and all these things shall be added to you."

For the first time, I really knew what that verse meant. I said, "Lord, that's it, isn't it? I'm supposed to be seeking You first, aren't I? Lord . . . help me to know how to do that."

Up to this point, I had been trying to use God to get what I wanted, instead of giving all that I had to God. I began to understand what it meant to really seek Him.

God's Word changed my entire perspective on life. I

began to want to get up in the morning and see what the day had in store. I began to set goals and pray for His strength and wisdom to achieve them. The Lord began a process in my life of "remaking" Eva. He used a lot of people as parts of the process teaching me how to put God's kingdom first and how to seek His righteousness above all things. One of the people He used the most was Mama.

began to want to get up in the morning and see what the day had in store. I began to set goals and pray for the strength and wisdom to achieve them. The Lord began a process in my life of "remaking" them. He used a lot of people as parts of the process teaching me how to put God's kingdom first and how to seek His righteousness above all things. One of the people He used the most was Mama . . .

12

Getting Back in the Game

❧

The L*ORD* *is my helper;*
I will not fear.
(Hebrews 13:6)

So many people tried to encourage me when I was in the hospital by saying, "Eva, you're special and you're going to make it!" "Eva, you're a fighter—you're not a quitter!" "Eva, if anybody can conquer this, you can! You've got the courage it takes!"

Those were some of the biggest lies ever told.

Now, the people who said these things to me didn't *mean* to lie. They thought they were encouraging me. But the facts were: I wasn't special, I wasn't a fighter, I *was* a quitter, and I wasn't all that courageous. Deep down inside, I'm one of the biggest wimps who has ever lived.

It's only after I've come to the conclusion that I've cried all the tears I can cry, I've had a fit, and I've thrown in the towel, that Jesus seems to walk over and pick up the towel I just threw in. He then rolls it up, flicks me with it, and says, "Eva, you've got to get back in the game."

In my recovery process, the time had come for Eva to get back in the game.

One day Mama came in and after she had helped me with a sponge bath and had helped me get into my back brace, she sat down in a chair near the bed and she handed me a pair of blue jeans. She said, "Eva, I want you to put these blue jeans on by yourself today."

I said, "Mama, I can't do that right now. I can't bend and twist enough. I'll get this back brace off in a couple of months and then I'll be able to put those jeans on by myself."

She said, "I think you can do it now."

I'm embarrassed to tell you how I responded to my mama. Basically, I ordered her out of my room.

Before she left, she went to the end of the bed and stretched out my jeans and put the top of them just over my toes with the legs of the jeans hanging down from the end of the bed.

After she had gone, I sat up and reached down and grabbed my jeans and pulled them up a little bit. I threw myself back down on the bed and cried. Then I sat up and made a second attempt and pulled and tugged at them some more. And again, I threw myself back down on the bed and cried a little more. I sat up a third time and tugged more, moving my body from side to side as much as I could to try to get those pants up over my hips. I fell back onto the bed, this time in exhaustion.

And as I lay there, I heard my mama crying. She had been in the next room the entire time. She had heard me struggling. And she was crying on my behalf.

I realized in that moment how difficult it was for her *not* to help me—in fact, it was more difficult for her *not* to help than it was to help. It caused her greater pain to see and hear me struggle.

Oh, I want to be a mama like that—to have the discernment to know when to help and when to allow my children to struggle and put their entire trust in God for *His* help.

I got those jeans on, transferred into my wheelchair, and wheeled myself into the next room and hugged my mama. I thanked her for what she had done.

So many times the Lord has given us all we need, but we don't recognize the sufficiency of His supply. He has given us His Word, all the resources and ideas we need, the ability to pray and to believe, the strength and energy to get through a day, friends to encourage us and family to love us.

He expects us to use what He has given us—and to put on our blue jeans. We cannot rely on others to do *for* us what God requires *of* us.

When we make the effort—even though it may take some pulling and tugging and crying—He will be faithful to help us. And all along the way, He will be compassionate in His love for us. The Lord doesn't send us out to do His work and ignore us until we come back with a good report. He's standing in the shadows all the time, weeping with us as we weep, rooting for us as we struggle, and rejoicing with us when we rejoice.

God expects us to do what we can do. And then to trust Him with those things that only He can do.

13

Bathtubs and Folding Machines

Why are you cast down, O my soul?
And why are you disquieted within me?
Hope in God, for I shall yet praise Him
For the help of His countenance.
(Psalm 42:5)

*B*athtubs and folding machines may not have anything to do with each other as far as most people are concerned. Yet, they seem directly connected in my life.

After I had managed to get my blue jeans on, the thought occurred that there were other things I could probably do. I was reading my Bible daily and talking to the Lord a lot by then. I was also memorizing a verse every week and reading *The Power of Positive Thinking.* The practical result was that each week, I decided that I was going to work on one specific skill and see how much I could do.

For example, one week I made up my mind that I was going to work on transferring from the living room sofa to my wheelchair, and back from the wheelchair to the sofa, without looking spastic. Another week I worked on transferring from my wheelchair into the bathtub. When I finally managed to get into the bathtub without falling, I sat there with all my clothes on in a dry tub, yelling, "Daddy, Daddy, come in here!"

He ran into the bathroom and I said, "Look, Daddy! I got in here all by myself!"

He said, "Girl, you've done gone *crazy.*"

I didn't let what he said faze me in the least. I said, "Watch me get out!"

Daddy watched me position myself and move my legs and get out of that tub. He was in a little bit of awe, I think. It was quite a maneuver. (Later, in college, the girls were so interested in seeing how I managed to get in and out of the bathtub that I felt like charging admission!)

My goal was to do things in fluid motions instead of jerky movements so that people wouldn't stare at me or feel sorry for me. Daddy watched me practice, usually with a negative, nervous look. He kept saying that he was afraid I was going to hurt myself. I finally explained to him that I was already paralyzed and the likelihood of my injuring myself any worse was slim to none!

I also practiced pushing myself in my wheelchair up and down the streets in our neighborhood. Daddy was sure that the hot rods that raced up and down our street were going to run over me. He'd chase me down the street as I rolled away from him as fast as I could, yelling for him not to push me. I was especially determined to roll up the hill myself.

After I had worked at Zayre's for several months, I finally had saved enough money to buy another car. Daddy went with me to pick it out. The car actually was his choice. I bought a '72 Mercury Montego—similar to the car on the *Starsky and Hutch* TV show—army green with a price tag of a thousand dollars. Daddy wanted a car that looked like a tank and drove like a tank so that it might protect his daughter like a tank. The Montego qualified.

It took me a couple more weeks to save enough money to have the car outfitted with the hand controls I needed. While I waited, I worked on getting in and out of the car by myself, and I practiced pulling my wheelchair into the backseat so I'd be ready to drive without anyone's help as soon as the car was outfitted. Daddy couldn't stand to watch me struggle with pulling that heavy wheelchair into the backseat once I was seated up front. He kept saying, "Girl, you can't do this by yourself. You've got to let me help you!"

Finally Mama came out in the yard to see what was happening. I told her that Daddy kept trying to help me and

I needed to learn how to get the wheelchair into the car by myself. She literally pulled Daddy back into the house by his ear and she called over her shoulder that if I needed any help to honk the horn.

It took me quite a while to learn how to manage that chair into the backseat, but once I figured it out, I was thrilled that I could go places on my own without any assistance.

And what does all this have to do with folding machines?

Much of what I was doing in those days was repetitious —hour after hour of practicing the same thing. Hour after hour of trying to get better at very simple skills. In lots of ways, it was like working in a factory.

Factory work was something Mama knew about all too well. By the time she retired, Mama had worked in the mill forty-four years, eight hours a day and sometimes overtime.

Mama usually rode the factory bus home from work so it was always a treat for her if someone picked her up at the mill. One afternoon when I was in high school I went to pick her up and on that particular afternoon, I was daydreaming as I sat in the mill parking lot waiting for the shift change. I was listening to the radio in my orange and white '74 Maverick. When the buzzer sounded and hundreds of people poured out of that big red brick factory, many of them almost ran for their buses or cars. It looked to me like a bunch of kids getting out of school for summer break.

I can only imagine what it must have been like for Mama to work in that factory, day after day, week after week, year after year. Every day was exactly the same— lunch at a certain time, breaks at certain times, and the sweet sound of a shift buzzer at exactly the same time every day. In all those years, I only heard Mama complain once about her job, however, and that was the day that the company introduced an "automated folding machine."

Mama had been folding sheets by hand for thirty-four years—from the time she was sixteen until she was fifty—when that machine was brought into the plant. Her new job was to feed this machine, which speeded up the folding process. And Mama wasn't sure she could do it.

Mama wasn't very coordinated and she was afraid she'd lose her job before she could learn how to load that beast. She shed countless tears and several times she said to me, "I've just got to figure it out. I've got to learn to do this." And in the end, she conquered the folding machine and operated it for ten more years until she retired.

Overcoming that folding machine was one of the biggest obstacles my mother ever faced. If I were in her situation today, I probably would say, "Well, I'm just going to get another job." Mama didn't see that as an option. She *had* to learn something that was very difficult for her to learn.

I remember talking to the Lord while I was trying to learn how to transfer into the bathtub, "Lord, where do I put my leg? Where do I put my right hand?" So much of learning how to live with paralysis is self-taught—you just have to figure it out for yourself. That's true for most things in life, I think.

We each have to face challenges and set goals related to them. We each have to practice until we "figure it out" and "get it right" in our lives.

I didn't want to try to get into the bathtub with paralyzed legs any more than Mama wanted a folding machine in her life. But we each figured out what to do, with God's help.

I don't know what you're facing in your life today that is a challenge to you. But I know this: there's a way to do it. And if you ask the Lord about it, I believe He'll show you the way.

14

A New Chapter

Do not remember the former things,
Nor consider the things of old.
Behold, I will do a new thing,
Now it shall spring forth.
(Isaiah 43:18–19)

eith had gone to Gardner-Webb College in the fall and one day he called me and said, "I was talking to the admissions director and he told me they were trying to make the campus accessible for students in wheelchairs. I told him about you and he gave me an application for you to fill out. I'm coming home this weekend and I'm going to bring this application over to you."

I gave Keith all of my usual excuses but Keith was persistent. The admissions director later came to my house to talk to me and Daddy. He talked about how I might be able to pay for college, and soon after that, he came and got me and we drove to the college together. As we toured the campus he asked me what needed to be done in various areas to make the campus accessible to me in my wheelchair and I gave him some suggestions.

Actually the campus looked pretty good to me. At home on Linden Avenue all we had done was put a piece of plywood at a slant over the front steps to make a ramp, and Daddy had put a metal bar in the bathroom to help me in getting in and out of the tub.

Finally, the admissions director and I went to his office and he put an envelope on my lap. Inside was a letter that said I had been accepted as a student at Gardner-Webb College. The only thing that stood in my way was retaking the SAT and I agreed to give it another try. The admissions director said to me, "Do us proud, Eva. Just do us proud."

I later went to a VIP weekend and stayed in the dorm. I

began to get more and more excited about going to college.

The day I left for college, I backed out of my driveway with Mama and Daddy waving both hands and both of them crying. I thought, *This is the dumbest thing I've ever done. I'm leaving all the security I have.*

I was a little intimidated to be starting in the middle of the school year, a full semester behind the rest of my class. Not only that, but I was also on academic probation.

I was concerned that I didn't have the right clothes to wear, and I was anxious about what the other girls would think of me. I wondered who would pull me up the steps into the buildings that didn't have a ramp. What if it rained and my chair got stuck in the mud? Would anybody ask me to go to a basketball game?

But then I remembered my first day of elementary school.

I vividly recall my first day of school. Mama couldn't go with me—she had to walk half a mile to catch the mill bus at six o'clock in the morning, and while Daddy usually was there for breakfast with us kids, he didn't take us to school. So it was up to my brother and me to get ourselves on our buses.

The night before the first day of school, Mama gave me lots of particulars. She told me that I was to wait patiently until the school bus came and that I wasn't supposed to wander off. She told me that I'd love school and it would be a wonderful experience and that I'd make lots of new friends and have fun things to do. She said we'd talk it all over when I got home. And she told me that Jesus would walk with me every step of the way.

That first day of school, Mama was sad that she couldn't

go with me. She came into my room before she left for work and I could tell she was crying. She said, "Eva, I'm sorry I can't go with you. But I want you to know that if you need anything or get scared about anything, just talk to the Lord."

I said, "Okay, Mama." If Mama told me to talk to Jesus if I had a problem, well, that was good advice and that's what I'd do. I felt fine about going to school on my own because Mama had instilled in me that Jesus was with me, and because He was with me, I really wasn't alone.

I never really thought about there being different buses for the high school and elementary school. I just assumed I'd go out and the first school bus that came along, I'd get on it.

Well, the first bus came by and I got on it—and then I got off it. It was the high school bus. My brother was angry that I hadn't waited for him. We were off to a rocky start— but I wasn't bothered in the least, not even by my brother's yelling.

My brother pushed me in the direction of the elementary school and one of the mothers took me under her wing and got me to the right door for my class. I looked around and all of the other kids seemed to have their mothers with them. Some of them were crying and some of their mothers were crying, too.

I felt really sorry for them. I thought, *These poor kids must not have Jesus with them. They need their mamas and even with their mamas here, some of them are crying.*

I'm grateful that Mama taught me early on that I was never alone. And on the drive to Gardner-Webb College, I had that same assurance fill my heart again. I wasn't alone.

Sometimes a person has to step out in faith to do what

he feels God is calling him to do. We can be assured that when we step out in faith and obedience, He is there for us. Jesus was, indeed, with me every mile of the way to Gardner-Webb.

15

College Days

*But You, O Lord, are a God full
of compassion, and gracious,
Longsuffering and abundant in
mercy and truth.
(Psalm 86:15)*

*B*eing the first student in a wheelchair at Gardner-Webb College turned out to be a much more positive experience than a negative one. It seemed every girl in school wanted to be my friend. The main reason? I was a "guy magnet." Because very few of the buildings on campus had ramps, I needed to be pulled up stairs several times a day. Usually a big, strapping guy came to my rescue and hauled me up to the classroom I needed to be in. My new girlfriends wanted to be right by my side so they could be seen by these big, strong guys!

One special guy was Jonathan Scott. He always helped me up the steps to our eight o'clock music theory class. He usually was leaning against the wall waiting for me to roll up. On mornings when I was running later than usual, he'd go ahead and take a seat in class. If he wasn't outside waiting for me, I'd throw a small rock against the glass of our classroom window as a signal for him to come out and get me. One morning, the windows were open and I could hear my professor lecturing. I threw several small rocks, but Jonathan didn't get the message. To my great embarrassment, I heard the professor stop his lecture and say, "Jonathan, I believe that's Eva. That's the third rock this morning!"

Another thing that made me popular on campus was the fact that I had a car. It wasn't the nicest or newest car, but it could hold a lot of people and it was a ticket to the freedom and adventures of going into town. The restaurants in Shelby were important to us college students. Other than the cafeteria, which was known for serving "mystery meat," the only places to eat within walking distance of the college were the Snack Shop and a place called Quick Snack. A person could only eat there so often!

One day six of us piled into my car on a quest for food. We stopped at the Pantry to put gas in the car and I was a little irritated at all the arguing among my friends about where we should go eat. I jerked the steering wheel to make a dramatic point as I zoomed away. Unfortunately, when the steering wheel jerked the car also jerked. One foot fell onto the gas pedal and the other slid under the brake pedal so the hand controls wouldn't work! The car lurched forward, with black smoke pouring out of the exhaust, and I began screaming, "I can't stop, I can't stop!" Three men were coming out of the Pantry and they looked up in horror at the sight of my big green Mercury Montego barreling down on them. They thought they were about to be mowed down.

The right front end of my car plowed through the storefront. The brick wall made the car stop. After the glass stopped falling on the roof of the car and the floor around the car, there was dead silence. The clerk stood frozen behind the counter in shock.

One of my friends then burst out laughing and said, "Eva, this is great! It's just like in the movies! Let's do it again!" Everybody climbed out to check the damage to the store and the car. The clerk had to climb over the hood of the car to get to the pay phone to call for help. It was comical to hear him explaining on the phone, "No, I'm not kidding. There really is a car sticking out of the front window."

I started crying because I knew Daddy was going to have a fit because I'd ruined the store and wrecked my car.

I just knew he'd never let me drive again and I'd have to drop out of school to pay for the damages.

When I got out of the car, I started crying even harder because there was amber-colored fluid everywhere and I assumed it was transmission fluid. That meant I really had ruined my car! I was wailing about my situation when my history professor came over to me. He bent down, touched the amber fluid with his fingers, and then smelled his hand. He said, "Eva, calm down. That's not transmission fluid. It's orange soda."

I had driven through a promotional pyramid display of orange soda bottles!

Insurance covered all the damages and I became known as the person who created the first drive-through window in Boiling Springs.

I had very few problems adjusting to college life. Perhaps the biggest challenges came the first few days of registration.

I had to decide upon a major. My roommate Susan was planning to be a music major and since I liked music, I decided that I'd be a music major, too. Susan and I went over together to meet Dr. Cribb, the department chair for the School of Music.

The meeting was a little embarrassing. The facts were— I didn't know which key was middle C on the piano, I didn't know how to read music, I didn't know that a guitar had six strings, and I didn't know the difference between a quarter note and a half note.

Dr. Cribb said, "Are you *sure* you want to major in music?"

I said, "I am!"

I told Dr. Cribb that I thought I could pick up those

things pretty fast if he'd just give me a chance. To my relief, he did. And to my amazement, I eventually graduated with a degree in music education.

My voice teacher, Miss Gregg, said to me at one of my first lessons, "Honey, you sing like a hick." But then she went on to say, "We're going to work on this."

I just said, "Yes, ma'am." The fact was, I was a hick. I was a simple mill-town girl who loved to sing the country songs her daddy and brothers had taught her. Miss Gregg actually had a great influence on my life. She knew when to back off and when to push me.

My second great challenge at the start of college had to do with textbooks.

I had thought that books were given to you in college just as they had been in high school. After we registered for classes, one of my new friends said, "Let's go freshen up in the dorms and then hurry over to the bookstore to buy our books. If we wait until after lunch, the bookstore will be packed."

I panicked. I didn't have any money for books. I only had ten dollars, no checking account, and no credit card. I had a work scholarship but I hadn't started working yet. I had applied for a loan from the college but had been told that all of the loan money had been given out and there wasn't any left for me to borrow because I was starting in the middle of the year. I had no idea what to do. Back in the dorm room, all alone, I told the Lord I was grateful for the few days I had enjoyed at college, but that it looked like now was the time for me to go home.

I started crying. And then I looked down at the floor and I saw an envelope there. Someone had put it under my door because I hadn't been assigned a post office box yet.

Inside was a thank-you note from a church where I had spoken a few days before . . . and with the note was an honorarium check. It more than covered the cost of my books. When my friends came back by my room and asked, "Are you ready, Eva?" I wiped my face and said, "Yes! I just need to know where I can get a check cashed first."

God constantly amazes me with the kindness He shows to His children. I never had to tell my new friends that I didn't know we had to buy our books or that I didn't have the money to buy them.

16

Fitting In and Reaching Out

*And we know that all things work together for good
to those who love God, to those who are the called
according to His purpose.*
(Romans 8:28)

itting in was very important to me. I wanted to be a "normal" student in every way possible. I especially hated it when it snowed. I felt stuck inside since my wheelchair couldn't make it through the snow.

Four of my friends came to my room and found me sitting there depressed one snowy day. They immediately began throwing hats and gloves at me, saying, "Put this on and put this on." All the while I was protesting, "I can't go out in the snow." They insisted I come with them outside and once I was there, they tied ropes onto my wheelchair and pulled me out into the snow as if I were in a sled. We went over to the boys' dorm and ended up in a huge snowball fight.

One of my friends said to one of the big ol' football players that came out for the fight, "Hit that girl in the wheelchair over there."

He said, "I can't do that."

She said, "Why not? Can't you throw that far?"

He said, "No, that's not it. I can't throw a snowball at her. She's not in good health."

My friend laughed and said, "Well, if you don't get her first, she'll get you!" And I did. We ended up going to my roommate Elizabeth's parents' house for hot chocolate later that afternoon and we had a great time.

Moments like that were really special to me because I felt totally like one of the group. That wasn't always the case.

I remember one time I went home with a guy I was dating. He was very sweet and very proud that he was dating me. He invited me home for a weekend to meet his parents.

I went to that home determined that I was going to impress the socks off his parents, especially his mother. She wasn't at all impressed with me.

The next morning, I had dressed and made my bed and was getting ready to leave the room when she walked in and threw some sheets on the bed and said, "Would you please put clean sheets on the bed, Eva?"

From the tone of her voice, I thought, *She's trying to pick a fight with me or hurt my feelings!* I said, "Okay" and I changed the bed.

My boyfriend was waiting for me when I finally rolled out into the living room and we headed for the kitchen. He said, "Mom, aren't you going to fix breakfast for us?" She looked at me and said, "Eva, there's the stove. There's the refrigerator. You can fix something."

I said, "That's all right. I don't usually eat breakfast" and I left it at that. I realized that this woman didn't approve of me one bit, solely because I was in a wheelchair, and she was doing everything possible to show her son all that I couldn't do in hopes of convincing him that I could never be a good wife or homemaker. She knew I couldn't reach the shelves or cupboards and that I couldn't fix his breakfast without help. She was right—there are some things that are difficult for a person in a wheelchair. But she was wrong about whether I was a person good enough for her son. I had learned, however, by living with Daddy and three big brothers and two foster brothers that a girl has to pick her fights carefully. This was one fight I could walk away from.

And then there were the preacher boys. Gardner-Webb is a Baptist college with many students who go on to seminary. Some of these guys thought I would be an "asset" to their public ministry. A woman who could sing, play the guitar, and who sat in a wheelchair—why, that was enough drama for a really large pastorate! I noticed that some of these guys were much more attentive to me if we were in a public place or they were trying to impress somebody. It was as if they wanted everyone to notice how kind they were to a girl in a wheelchair.

A wheelchair creates its own kind of spotlight. That can be good. When I went with my friends to witness on the boardwalk at the beach, I noticed that none of them drew very big crowds when they took the microphone. But when I rolled up in my wheelchair, people stopped to listen.

A wheelchair can also create a spotlight when you don't want one. And especially at times when other people try to jump in that spotlight.

I went with one boyfriend to Disney World and we seemed to draw a crowd wherever we went. He rode around on the back of my chair, splashed me in puddles, sat on my lap, and gave lots of the tourists a Kodak moment. But this same guy later told me that I could be in the spotlight anytime I liked, but he would never be in my shadow. He liked my wheelchair, but only if it worked for his benefit.

The more opportunities I had to be with people, the more opportunities I had to minister. Most of those opportunities were very positive. At the beginning, of course, I had very little idea what to do or "how" to minister.

Actually, a fairly high percentage of the guys at Gardner-Webb were preparing to become full-time ministers. They loved to preach in the small churches in the Boiling Springs area, and most of the small churches loved having young preacher boys in their pulpits. A few of these guys started inviting me to go on their speaking trips with them, usually to sing and play the guitar before they spoke. I discovered that music really has the capacity to touch people's hearts and there were lots of times when I thought later, *A song is sometimes even better than a sermon. A song can say it all.*

I remember the first time a student preacher asked me if I'd go with him to a church to give my testimony. I said, "Sure" and then I asked him what a testimony was! He said it was just the story of how I met Jesus and what God was doing in my life. Well, I didn't know much about theology, but I knew about telling stories. After all, I'd been telling stories from the time I could talk. I had learned by listening to Daddy.

Speaking at churches did more than just help me fit in. It helped me pay for my school expenses and it also taught me a wealth of other things about ministry. I learned that people like to be "talked with" instead of "preached at." I learned to eat whatever food the pastor's wife offered to me. I learned that most people are a little lonely and that everybody longs to be loved unconditionally.

I learned not to be distracted by church members who fall asleep. I learned that the most precious gift you can give another person is a reminder that God loves them.

I also learned that a wheelchair didn't handicap me in telling people about Jesus—in fact, it seemed to open some doors to people who probably wouldn't otherwise have listened to a girl from Concord.

It was the first time I began to see my paralysis as an *asset.* I feel sure there are lots of people who have never stopped to think that their biggest "problem" or "failure" can actually become the biggest asset in their lives. But with God involved, all things have a good side, and all things can work together for good. All things can become a blessing.

17

Two Steps Back and Three Steps Forward

*For our light affliction, which is but for a moment,
is working for us a far more exceeding and
eternal weight of glory.*
(2 Corinthians 4:17)

n March of my first semester at Gardner-Webb—just two months after I had started college—I discovered blood when I catheterized myself one morning. I didn't have much pain but I knew the blood wasn't a good sign so I went immediately to a urologist in town.

He checked me into the hospital, I called Mama and Daddy to tell them what I was doing, and the next day I had surgery to remove a kidney stone.

To my surprise, Mama and Daddy came to the hospital for the surgery and after I was released from the hospital, they visited the campus of my college for the first time. Both of them were intimidated, but I could tell they were also proud.

When I returned to campus, the financial aid officer called me. He asked me to come by as soon as possible. He informed me that someone had given an anonymous three-thousand-dollar donation to the college to help with my expenses. He couldn't tell me who gave the money, but the good news for me was that I didn't have to worry about tuition for a while. I was able to stay at Gardner-Webb. This happened several times during my years at the college and I never did find out who was writing the checks.

A week after my surgery I was back in class— transferring into and out of my wheelchair was painful, but I managed. I was able to finish the semester all right and with good enough grades that I was taken off probation. Things were looking up!

That summer I went to a Christian camp at the beach to

work. I loved Camp Caswell and the opportunity to hang out at the ocean for two months. The only problem was that I developed a fairly serious pressure sore on my tailbone. That kept me from being able to handle an active job so my job ended up being in the dining hall. I was responsible for cracking open all of the eggs used for breakfast—hundreds of them every morning! I got to the point where I could crack four eggs at one time, two in each hand! And then, during meals, I sat behind the counter and punched meal tickets. I got really sick of eggs that summer, but I loved getting to meet all of the campers in the meal line. I made it part of my job description to make the kids laugh and feel comfortable, regardless of how the food tasted.

Because of those chats in the meal line, I was invited to several of the cabins to give devotions. That was the first time many of the campers realized that I was in a wheelchair. I had always been sitting down behind a counter in the cafeteria line so they had no idea I couldn't walk. My wheelchair actually helped keep the attention of some of the kids as I told my story.

A number of these kids went home to their churches all over North Carolina and told their pastors about me. A few friendly visits in the cafeteria line led to my having speaking opportunities all over the state.

It was because of these invitations to speak that two of my friends—B. B. and a girl we nicknamed Gus—and I started the Rainbow Ministry. We drove to all of our engagements in my big green Montego and on the longer road trips, we usually challenged one another to harmonizing contests. As it turned out, Gus could harmonize with the car horn, so she usually won.

God weaves the threads of our lives into an amazing

tapestry at times. My tapestry was becoming more colorful month by month. I had a busy time at the end of the summer and all fall semester studying during the week and speaking and singing on weekends.

Unfortunately, although I kept my pressure sore very clean, I wasn't able to stay off it enough for it to heal. Part of the problem was that I was still very skinny. The end of my spine was so sharp and I was so thin, that tailbone just kept pushing through the skin. I made it through the fall semester but by January, the area was bleeding constantly. The doctor said, "Eva, if gangrene sets in, you might die." He didn't have to tell me twice. I agreed to a surgery to have the end of my spine shaved.

I had to lie on my stomach for nearly a month. That surgery brought back lots of memories of the first few weeks after my accident and the time I spent on the Stryker frame. I faced hours of hard physical therapy because in a month of inactivity, muscles can really atrophy. The days fell into a rather numb routine of playing cards and watching television.

The bright side of that semester was that a woman named Connie came into my life. Connie was the younger sister of a friend and she started visiting me every day. She had become involved with the wrong crowd in high school and had dropped out during her senior year. Even though she dropped out, she finished her GED exam and she had dreams of becoming a nurse. Her first visits to see me were primarily for research!

She asked questions about *everything* and she actually took over some of the more unpleasant tasks of my home nursing. She was very matter-of-fact and easygoing, and rather than make me feel embarrassed, she seemed grateful for the chance to get some practical nursing experience. I discovered in Connie one of those rare people who can serve others without needing any recognition or applause. We became great friends.

She introduced me to soap operas. I introduced her to Christian television and Amy Grant music.

During that semester at home, I discovered how much I missed college. I had come to really enjoy studying, especially my music courses, and I had a strong desire to go back to Gardner-Webb. I was glad that I was well enough by summer to go to summer school. Connie went also. In the summer sessions, students had lessons every day rather than every week, so I made great progress in voice and piano.

It was during that summer session that I made three great friends, Laura, Mary, and Elizabeth. Laura and Mary were very active in the Fellowship of Christian Athletes, partly to meet the guys that belonged to FCA and partly because they enjoyed the activities. They began to talk to me about going with them to FCA meetings once the fall semester began.

Well, that fall Laura didn't return to school because she had been diagnosed with leukemia. One of the big social events at the start of the school year was the opening FCA meeting. I went, but I wasn't sure I was going to continue to go to the meetings. Laura called me from her home while she was in the middle of her chemotherapy treatments to insist that I continue to go to the FCA meetings, and because of my friendship and love for her, I did.

I became quite active in FCA and I made a whole new group of friends at Gardner-Webb. Little did I know at the time that I was also laying a foundation for later in my life.

18

y Leg Moved

He knows the secrets of the heart.
(Psalm 44:21)

One of my favorite classes was New Testament. It was the only course I failed and had to retake while I was in college, but I loved the class!

One day I wasn't paying very close attention to Dr. Prevost's lecture. Instead, I was staring at my leg and willing it to move. The therapists at the rehabilitation hospital had encouraged us to practice mental concentration so I was taking that opportunity to practice. I was furrowing my brows, concentrating on moving my leg, and suddenly, my leg moved! I couldn't believe it! I whispered to my friend Mary Ruth, "My leg moved."

She whispered back, "You're kidding!"

I said, "No, I'm not, watch this," and again, my leg moved.

Several students around us started to watch Mary Ruth and me and Dr. Prevost eventually noticed that we weren't paying attention. He said, "Eva, Mary Ruth, I want you two to turn around and pay attention right now."

I said, "Dr. Prevost, I'm not lying. I just moved my leg."

He stopped lecturing and walked over to my desk and told me to close my eyes. By now the rest of the class had gathered around my desk too.

Then he said, "Eva, I want you to move your leg now."

I concentrated really hard and my leg moved.

The whole class gasped and then several people started cheering and a few started crying.

Dr. Prevost asked me to do it again and I did.

He dismissed class for the day because he didn't think

we could concentrate on the lecture and celebrate a miracle at the same time!

I secretly began to hope that I'd continue to be able to control the movement of my legs and that perhaps I'd begin to have feeling in them and be able to walk. I knew that the therapists and physicians had said that some feeling and muscle ability can come back within a three-year period after a spinal cord injury. I didn't have any feeling, but I did have very limited movement in one leg—unfortunately, that's all it was.

Several of my friends told me of dreams they had in which I was walking or running. It was a heady time for us. We were full of enthusiasm about God's power. We just didn't understand that His ways are above ours and His miracles aren't always seen with the naked eye.

When I first arrived at Gardner-Webb College, I remember looking out over the campus and thinking, *I'm going to* walk *off this campus someday.*

By the time I graduated, I had accepted the fact that I wasn't going to walk off the campus, or walk anywhere. The chair was going to be a part of my life for the rest of my life unless God intervened in a very dramatic way directly or through medical miracles.

The main reason I believe I held on to my belief that I just *had* to be able to walk again someday was that I could not imagine living a full and meaningful life in a wheelchair. At that time, I couldn't imagine being married or having children as a paraplegic.

As the months went by, I came to realize that those people who had dreams about my walking were people who had just come to see *me* for who I was. They didn't see the chair any longer—they saw Eva.

And that pretty much was what happened to me, too, during my years at Gardner-Webb College. I began to regain a sense of who I was *apart* from my wheelchair. At the very beginning after my accident, I couldn't imagine myself in a wheelchair—all of my identity was as a person who didn't need a wheelchair. And then for a period I saw myself as a person *in* a wheelchair—a person who didn't have any identity other than as a "cripple." At this third stage, I saw myself as Eva, a loved and forgiven child of God, a work of God still in progress, a woman with all sorts of needs and desires and hopes and dreams—none of which had anything to do with a wheelchair one way or the other.

In my dreams today, I often see myself walking. Sometimes I see myself in a chair. Both of those people are *me*. And it's the real Eva that God is most concerned about and that I'm concerned about.

I believe that what happened to me happens to lots of people at some point in their life. They define themselves by their outward circumstances—good or bad—but the day comes when they have to say, "I'm not defined by this circumstance. God is defining me. My divorce . . . my social status . . . my bank account . . . my children . . . my husband . . . my job . . . yes, even my wheelchair . . . don't define me. My definition is that I am a forgiven, beloved child of God.

It's only when we allow God to define us—to make us and mold us and fashion us—that God truly can use us for His glory.

19

Homecoming Queen

*Now may the God of peace Himself sanctify you
completely; and may your whole spirit, soul,
and body be preserved blameless at the
coming of our Lord Jesus Christ. He who
calls you is faithful, who also will do it.*
(1 Thessalonians 5:23–24)

*D*uring my senior year, I was sitting on a ledge by the dorm one October afternoon singing a gospel song with a friend when a guy named Milton walked by and said, "I voted for you, Eva."

I said, "Thank you. You're so sweet."

He said, "I hope you win!"

I said, "I hope so, too."

As he walked away, I turned to Gus and said, "What's he talking about?"

Gus giggled and told me that I was running for homecoming queen. I said, "Yeah, sure. Do I look like a homecoming queen?"

She said, "No, Eva, but we thought it would be fun!"

She then told me that she and some of my other friends had passed around a petition and had signed me up secretly. By the time I found out what was going on, I had already won a runoff vote!

Homecoming is big-time at Gardner-Webb College. They roll out the red carpet in Boiling Springs on homecoming day. They import all the fancy cars in the area—two Corvettes. I was informed that I should wear a dress, which was a little foreign to me, since I had never worn a dress to a football game. So there I was, in my fancy dress, sitting on the back of this car. I don't have very good balance and the car was covered with balloons, which were flapping me in the face as we drove down the streets of Boiling Springs. My friends were lining the streets and calling to me as I passed by, "Eva, are you having fun? Are you having fun, girl?"

I remember pointing back at them as we drove by,

holding on for dear life and trying to keep the balloons out of my face at the same time and saying, "I'm gonna kill you when this is all over!"

When we got to the stadium, my escort was waiting. I was proud that my escort was my daddy. I'm not sure he knew what was going on but I think my girlfriends loved his being there.

Daddy was the only one who wasn't wearing a suit. He had on a flannel button-down shirt, blue pants, and a multicolored hat. He was nervous because he didn't know where to go and wasn't sure how to push me onto the field, plus he couldn't hear the directions very well since he was hard of hearing. In spite of my concern, Daddy got me to the right place on the field. The next thing I knew, an announcement was coming from a big white box, which was the public address system, and the words were, "And the 1982 Gardner-Webb College homecoming queen is . . ." After a long drum roll, I heard, "Miss Eva Whittington!"

People began going crazy. Some people looked as if they were having heart attacks. I myself felt as if I were having a heart attack!

A coach from a local high school was there with a group of boys and he began to watch their reactions to the announcement. In particular, he began to watch one little boy who had a big bag of popcorn. The boy was jumping up and down and throwing popcorn up in the air, yelling, "Yea, Eva! Yea, Eva!" Another little boy next to him was also jumping up and down. He finally said, "Hey, who's Eva?"

The first little boy turned to him and said, "What? You don't know Eva? I can't believe you don't know Eva. Everybody knows Eva." Then he paused and said, "Eva . . . is a Christian."

A few weeks later I was to speak at Coach Drake's high school and Coach Drake introduced me by telling that story. I thought, *Lord, that little boy doesn't know me, does he? He doesn't see me every day. But he must have seen something. It may have only been a little bit, but that something must have reminded him of You. What an honor, what a privilege to be associated with the King of kings and Lord of lords!*

It had been six years since Keith had told me to read my Bible and I had surrendered my entire life to Jesus. I knew I hadn't done everything right in those six years—in fact, I'd done some things completely wrong. But what I had done or not done was really not the issue. What *Jesus* was doing in me was all that mattered, and it still is all that matters.

It's all that matters in your life, too.

20

A Parting of the Red Sea

Every beast of the forest is Mine,
And the cattle on a thousand hills.
(Psalm 50:10)

was ready to get out of college but I also didn't know what in the world I'd do after I graduated.

When I finished college, I had three job offers. One was an opportunity to work as a minister of music at a church, the second was an opportunity to work as executive director for Handicapped Organized Women, and the third was to work as an area representative with the Fellowship of Christian Athletes. The FCA job was the one that appealed to me the most.

I decided to accept the job with FCA because it allowed me to use my musical background in an athletic setting. I was hired on a temporary basis for six months with the understanding that if the trial period went well, I would be hired permanently.

During my probationary period, I went to an FCA summer camp and shared my testimony with about a thousand high school boys. They were very responsive—they cried and cheered and gave me a standing ovation. Up to that point, I think some of the "old guard" in FCA considered me a risk. After all, I was in a wheelchair and I was a woman. I could understand their reservations! But the day after I shared my testimony at this camp, the FCA regional director asked me to accept a permanent position. I was thrilled to be an "official" part of the full-time staff of FCA.

FCA is like a lot of parachurch organizations—it requires its staff members to raise their own support. That first year, I had three weeks to raise $15,000. I didn't know anybody who had $15,000 . . . but then again, I did. I knew the One who has cattle on a thousand hills. (See Ps. 50:10.) I said, "Lord, if You want me to have this job, You know who has the money. Either lead them to me, or lead me to them."

It seems the Lord always makes us sweat a little. Perhaps He's trying to build our faith. Up until the last few days, I hadn't raised a penny. But then on the last day a man wrote a check for a thousand dollars, and another man wrote a check for $14,000. People say that God doesn't part Red Seas anymore . . . but I know He does.

The man who wrote the $14,000 check became a dear friend and supporter. His name is Robin Hayes. The first time I met Robin I was nervous. He didn't exactly grow up on my side of town, but he put me at ease right away. Robin showed up wearing jeans, a flannel shirt, and boots. He was driving a muddy vehicle and in all ways, he looked like a man who had just come in from hunting, which he probably had. He took me to Po' Folks for lunch and we talked about my experiences with FCA and what FCA meant to me and we had a great time. I completely forgot about the differences between us—the only thing that mattered to both of us was helping kids and their coaches to grow in their relationships with the Lord.

Through the coming months, Robin and his family helped a great deal behind the scenes in arranging for the various meetings and weekend activities that established FCA in the Concord area.

Robin was not only a great friend and financial supporter, but he taught me important life lessons. I had grown up with a terrible prejudice against rich people. I had been taught as a child that Jesus grew up poor and that He was a poor man as an adult. I had grown up poor. Poor was good! And because of that, rich wasn't all that good. Robin Hayes broke down a lot of my prejudice against rich people.

It wasn't only the fact that he had shown up for our first meeting in a plaid shirt and a dirty truck. Robin's attitude was always genuine and sincere. He taught me that a person should never be measured by their bank account, but by what is in their heart.

One time when Robin and I were riding together to an FCA banquet in Raleigh, I shared with him some of my prejudice about rich people. I told him how difficult I found it to raise funds at these banquets. He said, "Eva, you know what? Rich people are going to hell, too. Who do you think is going to reach them?"

I said, "I sure hope you are, Robin, because I'm not sure I can."

He said, "I think we can reach them together."

Robin never flaunted his wealth. It was quite a while before I ever saw his house. It was years before I knew he had a plane. It wasn't that Robin was trying to hide those things from me—they just weren't important for him to parade. And I learned from Robin that rich people can be generous, they can love the Lord, and they can be sensitive and obedient to the Lord.

In all ways, I loved working for FCA. It was neat to roll into schools all over the southern and central areas of North Carolina to meet kids and coaches on behalf of the Lord. I mainly worked in five rural counties and I never got tired of traveling around and talking to people about their relationship with Christ.

I can't remember all of the names of the kids I met, but I remember their faces.

I remember big, tough football players with tobacco tins

in their back pockets who asked me if God could really love them.

I remember fifteen-year-old girls with hard hearts and too much makeup who knelt before the Lord hoping that He could make them pure again.

I remember coaches who won all their games but were losing their families—coaches who changed their priorities after an encounter with the Lord.

I remember how hard it was to try to get a few minutes of sleep on a gym mat in a high school cafeteria during an all-night FCA Girls Lock-in with a hundred and fifty hyperactive teenage girls who had no concept of sleep deprivation.

And most of all, I remember how God showed Himself again and again to be the One who not only can start a work in the human heart, but also finish it for His glory.

21

Opportunities

My God shall supply all your need
according to His riches in glory
by Christ Jesus.
(Philippians 4:19)

orking for the Fellowship of Christian Athletes opened opportunities for me to speak in other parts of the country. I enjoyed the travel and making friends in new places.

One of the opportunities I experienced came through Hal Norton, the preacher who ran Garden City Chapel in South Carolina. I had spoken at the South Carolina state FCA convention, which was held at Garden City Chapel, a Christian summer outreach near Myrtle Beach. When I went out to pack my car, Reverend Norton came to me in the parking lot and asked, "Eva, why don't you record an album?" I told him there were two reasons: the first reason was that I didn't have the money, and the second reason was that I wasn't sure my heart was right.

Reverend Norton told me to get my heart right and he'd worry about the money.

A few months later, he called me and invited me to speak at one of his services. Right before I spoke, he told the congregation that he had never let anyone else speak in "his" pulpit before. I felt a little added pressure that this was such a big deal for him, but I appreciated the opportunity to share my story.

After I spoke, Reverend Norton gave an invitation for people to make a public confession of faith in Jesus Christ and then he walked over, put his arm around me, and told everyone that I was going to record an album and I needed $10,000. I was more surprised than anybody there to hear that I was going to record an album and I needed that much money to do it! That morning Reverend Norton collected

$4,000 for the album and he had the rest of the money a few months later.

It took a lot longer for me to figure out how to record the album than it took to raise the money. I think the main reason was because my heart wasn't in the right place yet. I was more excited about having my name on a record than I was about singing for God's glory.

Two years and a lot of heart lessons later, we got started. God worked in an amazing way.

My old college friend Jonathan Scott—the one who pulled me up the steps to music theory class—was the obvious person to produce the album. Jonathan is extremely gifted.

We recorded the album in a Miami studio in less than a week. Jonathan wrote seven songs for the album. He knew me so well—my voice and musical ability as well as my heart—that he knew just the right message for this recording.

I discovered through that entire experience that God always surrounds us with people whose strengths balance our weaknesses. He puts us together in ways we could never engineer on our own.

It was a lesson I had first seen in Mama's life.

Mama had a reputation for kindness. There was something in her that drew other people to her. She didn't always have a lot to give in the way of material or tangible things, but Mama was always generous with what she had.

Some of her friends at the mill came over and took her out and bought her some clothes and some things for me when I was just a baby. Mama was thrilled. I don't think anybody had ever done something so nice for her.

Mama grew up in a home with ten children so there were never very many things she could call her own, and even fewer things that were "new" and her own. It was special for her to have a new dress, and especially one from a store. It was special for her to know that her baby girl had nice things.

Again and again, other people met needs in Mama's life without her asking. Again and again, I was seeing the Lord use other people to meet needs in my life, too.

I am not saying that making a recording was a need in my life, but when the opportunity presented itself, God provided Reverend Norton, Jonathan, and all of the other resources necessary to glorify Him through this project. To God be the glory! Great things He has done, is doing, and will continue to do—in my life, and also in yours!

22

riends

There is a friend who sticks closer than a brother.
(Proverbs 18:24)

One Saturday the Fellowship of Christian Athletes had FCA Day at Six Flags Over Texas. You may never have been to an amusement park with a person in a wheelchair, but you might want to try it some time. I don't have to wait in line. I go right up the "Exit" lane and I get on the ride immediately—along with any friends who may be with me. And then, at the end of the ride, the attendant usually asks, "Would you like to ride twice?" And the friend who is in the car with me usually says, "We would." And so we go again.

Two rides without waiting—on any attraction I wanted to ride! I made a lot of new friends that day . . . in fact by the time I went on my fourth ride that day—it happened to be the "Swings"—I had seven new friends! And my new friends seemed to enjoy those rides as much as I did.

Good friends are important. My friends meet a lot of needs in my life, and if the friendship truly is working right, I am meeting needs in their lives as well.

I flew to Indiana one time to speak at a convention. My good friend Jona picked me up and drove me to the hotel. After we had checked into the hotel, we hooked up with two other gals—my friend Cindy and a new friend I had just met, Linda—and decided we'd go out together for something to eat.

Jona told us to go on out and get in the car while she ran back up to our room for something, so Cindy, Linda, and I went out to her car. I thought, *I've been riding in the front seat all the time. I'll let someone else ride in the front seat this time.*

I have a little trouble transferring from my wheelchair into a backseat. I can make that transfer without difficulty on my own into the front seat of a car, but not into the backseat. I explained to my friends how to help me and Linda got under my arms and Cindy under my knees and they got me into the backseat without any problem. We closed the door and left the wheelchair outside since we didn't have the key to Jona's trunk.

Linda climbed into the backseat with me and Cindy got into the front seat and we started talking. Talking seems to be a gift that women have. We can talk to near total strangers as if we've known them for years.

There are times when my friend Lisa and I get together and my husband, Andrew, asks, "Who listens?" We both can talk and listen at the same time. I try to tell Andrew, "It's a *gift*—from the *Lord*." But he's still amazed that we both can talk at the same time and yet still come away knowing fully what the other person said.

Well, after a few minutes of talking with Linda and Cindy, I began to wonder what was taking Jona so long. We continued talking and several more moments went by. All the while, I was scanning the parking lot looking for Jona. Finally I spotted her. She seemed to be looking for us.

Our eyes met and then she began to speak. I could read her lips because what she was saying was what *I* was saying —we were both speaking at the same time even though we couldn't hear each other. And what we were saying was . . . "W-r-o-n-g c-a-r."

I said again to my friends, "We're in the wrong car."

Cindy got all excited. "Wrong car? Did you say wrong car? Wrong car, wrong car, we're in the wrong car!" She opened up the front door, got out, and walked away! Cindy wasn't about to be in the wrong car!

I began to jump up and down a bit myself. "Linda, we're in the wrong—we're in the wrong car!" And Linda went into a pretty good Barney Fife imitation without really meaning to—she began to say, "What do ya want me to do, Eva? What do ya want me to do?"

I said, "You've got to get me out of the backseat of this car, Linda." So Linda opened the door on her side, got out, ran around the car, opened the door, scooped me up and threw me into my wheelchair, and off we went as fast as we could go.

Jona hadn't moved an inch—she would have come to help, I know she would have—if she hadn't been laughing so hard. When we finally got to her and Cindy, Cindy said, "I can't believe you got us into the wrong car, Eva. I am so embarrassed."

But mostly I was relieved that we hadn't been caught in the wrong car. We went through the same routine, only this time in Jona's car. Linda got into the backseat with me and Cindy got into the front seat—I wasn't talking too much to Cindy right then.

As we were preparing to pull out of the parking lot, we saw a man come out of the hotel and walk over to the car that we had been in. If he had walked out just a couple of minutes earlier, we truly would have been embarrassed. Of course, at that moment we were laughing too hard to be embarrassed—or anything else for that matter.

Do you have friends like Jona who can laugh *with* you at the embarrassing times in your life—knowing that she won't mind at all when you laugh *with* her at times she's embarrassed?

Do you have friends like Cindy who in a crisis seem to think mostly about themselves? Unfortunately, I am afraid that I have been that kind of friend at times.

Do you have a friend like Linda, who is right there with you, asking what she can do to help and refusing to leave your side?

Our friends come in lots of personalities but the important thing about our friends is how we relate to one another. A friend is a friend if you can share both good times and bad times with that friend, and if that friend stands by you no matter what happens.

There have been times in my life when I wondered if Jesus was a friend who disappeared quickly in a crisis, somebody who didn't seem truly to care about *my* problems or *my* hurts. But Jesus always stays close. He never leaves or abandons us. He is the Friend who sticks closer than a brother or sister—He is the Friend of all friends.

The more I have studied the Bible, the more I have realized that Jesus was different things to the different people He met.

To Peter, He was the Christ, the Son of the living God.

To Paul, He was the bright light who blinded him on the road to Damascus.

To John the Baptist, He was the Lamb of God.

To Mary and Martha, He was the Resurrection and the Life.

To Mary and Joanna and Mary Magdalene, He was the resurrected Christ.

To the Samaritan woman at the well, He was the living Water.

I began to question, "Who is Jesus to Eva?"

He is my best Friend.

When I'm scared, He is my security.
When I'm in despair, He is my hope.
When I'm depressed, He is my comfort.
When I have questions, He is the answer.
Jesus said, "I will never leave you. I'll never forsake you. I will never abandon you. I'll be there for you." He's been true to His Word in my life. And I know He'll be true to His Word for you, too.

23

Cancer

He Himself has said,
"I will never leave you nor forsake you."
(Hebrews 13:5)

moved to Charlotte two years after I started with FCA as a regional representative. I lived with Becky Bowman who was the head volleyball coach at the University of North Carolina in Charlotte. We first met each other at an FCA summer camp and we have a special friendship that lasts to this day.

Becky taught me how to create a filing system, and how to organize my job and my life.

She taught me how to cook Chinese food.

She taught me to value people, regardless of their position in life.

She taught me how to serve.

But the lesson for which I am most thankful is the lesson Becky taught me about "just being there" for a person in need. Becky walked with me through the most difficult period in my life. No, the paralysis from an automobile accident isn't what I consider to be the worst thing I have ever experienced. The worst thing was Mama's cancer.

I went to Concord one September to visit a junior high school and I called Mama from the school office to see if I could take her to lunch. She said she'd like that.

I then asked her how her doctor's visit had gone. She had been suffering from a cough that she couldn't seem to get rid of and the doctor had given her several medications but none of them had seemed to help. Mama said that her doctor had told her he wanted her to see a specialist in Charlotte because he suspected she had lung cancer. Mama was crying on the phone as she told me this and I told her I was hanging up because I was on my way—I'd be right there.

I wheeled out to my car. It was a warm day, but the leaves were already starting to turn. I remember thinking, *It's such a pretty day. I shouldn't be so sad.* But then I started sobbing. I begged God, "Please don't take my mama, please don't take my mama." Then for some reason, I calmed down and asked God to give me five more years with Mama.

The doctors in Charlotte confirmed that Mama had lung cancer. The mass was the size of an orange and it was inoperable. Mama began radiation and chemotherapy almost immediately.

From the time Mama was a young teenager, she smoked cigarettes. For her generation smoking cigarettes was considered glamorous and smoking was about the only "glamorous" thing Mama could afford to do in her life. I shouldn't have been shocked that Mama had lung cancer but nevertheless, I *was* shocked.

Becky and I both scheduled our lives around Mama's treatments because she couldn't drive and because we wanted to be with her anyway. We took turns driving her to and from Charlotte Presbyterian Hospital.

Becky and I both noticed changes in Mama's personality during the rides to and from the hospital and the long hours spent in the waiting room. Mama became hopeless, angry, depressed, bitter. She began to say cynical, hateful things. When I'd say to her, "Mama, there's no need to talk that way," she'd begin to cry. It was the first time I had ever seen Mama respond to life that way.

I finally decided we needed to talk to the hospital chaplain about the change in Mama's personality. He was very helpful.

Mama and I went together to see him. It was the first and only "therapist" Mama ever visited. He compared her situation to my accident and he reminded Mama how difficult it had been for her to watch me go through the various stages of my rehabilitation. He said, "Now your roles are reversed. May Bell, you are going to need to struggle through this on your own and work this out with the Lord." He pointed out to me that my role was to support her as she came to grips with what she was facing. One piece of advice that the chaplain gave Mama was this: "Get a reason for getting up in the morning."

Mama had always been good at crocheting. She probably made hundreds of doilies and little crocheted baskets in her life. Mama set a goal for a certain number of doilies and baskets she was going to crochet each week. When I got married, I had doilies all over the house—my husband had never seen doilies before and one day he came to me and said innocently, "Eva, what *are* these things all over the house?"

I said, "They're doilies! Haven't you ever seen a doily before?"

He said, "No." And then he asked, "What are they for?" That was a good question. I had never stopped to wonder what they were *for*. I just knew that Mama made them and we had a lot of them!

When Mama went for doctors' appointments, she crocheted little Christmas ornaments. She'd put them up on the counter when she paid her bill and people around her would usually start oohing and aahing over them. When somebody said, "These are so cute!" Mama would respond, "I'm selling 'em. I make 'em and sell 'em." And she'd make some money when she went for radiation and chemotherapy treatments!

It was very difficult for me to watch Mama go through this time. Mama had taught me to pray and to believe that God was faithful in all things. Mama had always been my spiritual anchor. No matter how tough the time, Mama's faith had been strong. It scared me to see her question God and to begin to stumble in her faith. Not only did I pray for God to restore Mama's health, but I started praying that He would strengthen her faith.

One of the hardest things I have ever done was to back off and let Mama work through her relationship with the Lord and her cancer on her own. I wanted to get in and "fix" things. I wanted to "make things right."

I knew then how much Mama had probably wanted to do the same for me after my accident. The only person to whom I could turn for advice on *how* to help Mama struggle on her own was . . . Mama. Mama was the one who had taught me what genuine independence was all about.

I don't remember my parents coming to my county ensemble performances, my ball games, or to see me as a cheerleader. I was in school plays and sang solos in church, but Daddy and Mama didn't go to those events. It may have been that I didn't invite them or because they didn't feel comfortable. I don't really remember. What I do know is that I participated in these events because I wanted to and because I felt confident in being on stage and on the basketball court. I didn't need their moral support because I had an inner strength that the Lord was with me and I could do these things on my own.

I've seen a lot of young people be pushed into events because their parents wanted them to be in those events. I'm grateful that wasn't the case with me. In many ways, Mama gave me wings — she gave me an independent spirit to make my own choices and to know that as long as I was honoring the Lord with my life, He would be with me no matter where I was or what I was doing.

Now when I began to give my testimony in churches, Mama rarely missed being there to support me. Daddy even came occasionally although he was always uncomfortable because I was speaking in a church. Mama's priorities were based on what was important to the Lord.

That doesn't mean that Mama didn't support my cheerleading, basketball, drama activities, or the other events in which I was involved. Mama always made my green and gold cheerleading outfits and I think she was happy that I was a cheerleader. It just wasn't something that was important for her to see me do. Her support was "behind the scenes."

I learned a lot from that. I learned that it's important to help another person, and especially our children, to feel grounded and confident *in the Lord*—not in their own strength but in the fact that the Lord is with them to help them in and through all things. It's also important to allow other people and our children to do what they desire to do in their lives. They aren't on this earth to fulfill our agendas but to fulfill their own dreams and goals. And as long as those goals are in line with God's Word, they are good goals and worthy of their effort.

In Mama's battle with cancer, I had to learn to trust Jesus in ways I never had before. I had to trust Him to do His work and to be with Mama apart from anything I did or said. I also had to trust Mama to trust God.

A friend of mine says that doubts are the growing pains of the soul. I believe that's true. Cancer left scars on Mama's life as a whole, but over time, Mama worked her way through her depression and bitterness. She decided that the one thing that she could continue to do just as well as she had ever done it was to pray. She found a way for her life to count *even with cancer.* And every Sunday Mama walked down the aisle at church and knelt at the altar to pray for two things: for Daddy to get saved and for me to get married. Believe me, Mama was praying for *miracles!*

24

Let Any Man Come

O Lord . . . blessed are those who trust in you.
(Psalm 84:12 TLB)

took the job with the Fellowship of Christian Athletes because I knew it was God's will for me. But I have to admit, I also had an ulterior motive. I just knew that within that organization, there had to be a good-looking Christian guy who would want to marry me.

I was right!

The only problem was that the guys who wanted to marry me didn't happen to be guys that *I* wanted to marry.

Some of my friends came to me shortly after I went on staff with FCA and they said, "Eva, do you know why you aren't married?"

I said, "Because I need to lose weight and grow fingernails?"

They said, "No . . . it's because you aren't claiming the Scriptures." Now, please understand that this may not be good theology and if you are single and reading this, please take it in the spirit in which it is intended. This advice may not be for you. My friends, however, were very serious when they told me, "Eva, you need to get a verse, claim it, and pray it to the Lord."

They kept pushing me on this and they kept asking me if I had a verse. One day I told them I had found a verse— "If any man will come . . . let him" (Matt. 16:24 KJV).

A few years later, I found another verse that seemed appropriate given the experiences I had been having with dating: "All men are liars" (Ps. 116:11).

In all seriousness, Psalm 84:11 was the verse that I finally claimed in my heart:

The LORD will give grace and glory;
No good thing will He withhold
From those who walk uprightly.

That verse said several things to me—it said that the *Lord* is the One who gives us those things that allow us to reveal His grace and glory to the world. It said that the Lord wouldn't withhold anything from me that was a *good thing* for me. And it said that if I were walking uprightly before the Lord—seeking to do things His way and trusting Him with my entire life—He would see that I had everything I needed to fulfill His plan and purpose for my life.

That's encouraging to me! No matter how slow or dull I might be—even if I don't "get it" right away—I won't miss out on what the Lord has for me. He will make sure that I receive the good things He has for me.

When it came to my precious husband, Andrew, I was a little slow and I didn't quite "get it" at first . . . but I didn't miss out. The Lord knew the desires of my heart for a godly husband and precious children, and He had a plan. I only needed to walk uprightly and seek "first" His kingdom, and in His time He would reveal His plan to me.

Andrew and I first met in 1985 when I spoke at the Kentucky State FCA Convention. Andrew was in his senior year at Centre College, a small liberal arts college in Danville, Kentucky. He was captain of the football team and very active in FCA. He seemed like a nice, sincere, Christian guy, but I was dating someone else at the time and never really thought much more about him. He went on to law school and I went on with my life as an FCA staffer in North Carolina.

A couple of years later, our paths crossed again and I

ended up riding with him to the Kentucky State FCA Convention. At that time, we both had just broken off what we thought were serious relationships. We shared each other's pain and attempted to comfort each other, although I don't believe that either of us was successful.

At that particular conference, I found some time to play tennis with my friends Lynnette and Alice. I was trying to get good enough at wheelchair tennis to beat my old boyfriend. But we had only three tennis balls among us and chasing them got old pretty quick. Andrew saw us playing and spent an entire afternoon shagging balls for us. After we finished playing, Alice called a huddle with Lynnette and me. She put her arms around our shoulders and said, "Okay, y'all. One of us is going to have to marry this guy because he's too good to let him get away."

Lynnette, who was a good friend of Andrew's and on staff with FCA in Kentucky, grinned at me and I immediately said, "No way, Lynnette. Don't start that again." Lynnette had told me a year earlier that she thought Andrew really liked me and that he would be a good catch. I thought Andrew was a great guy, really smart, and fun . . . I wasn't sure, however, if I could ever trust another man.

Everybody else seemed to have no difficulty trusting Andrew. One time, my friend Becky went on a recruiting trip to Lexington, Kentucky—Andrew went to law school at the University of Kentucky in Lexington. Lynnette, who also lived in Lexington, invited them both to dinner. When Becky came home, she told me she had met the man I was going to marry. I said, "Don't tell me . . . Andrew Self."

In the months and years that followed, I saw Andrew a few times at FCA events, and I continued to believe that he was a "jewel" of a guy, but I just didn't see us as a couple.

Then, in May of 1988, after Andrew had finished law school and before he began studying for the Bar exam, he came to see me in Concord. He explained to me that he was going to visit his brother in Florida and that he wanted to stop by and see me on his way back to Kentucky. Since I didn't know my geography very well, I assumed that North Carolina was on the beaten path from Florida to Kentucky. I had no idea Andrew had driven hundreds of miles out of his way just to see me.

As dull as I was about some things, it was pretty obvious that Andrew really liked me. I had just started dating someone else at the time Andrew came to visit me. I still considered him a good guy and friend, but that was all.

Later that summer, our paths crossed yet again at an FCA camp at Black Mountain, North Carolina. Andrew and some of his Kentucky FCA buddies rode their bikes three hundred miles just to get to the camp. I found out later that one of the main reasons Andrew came to Black Mountain that summer was to see me, even though he was studying for the Bar exam at that time. However, throughout the week, we seldom had time to visit with each other. One thing was sure—Andrew had heard the rumors that I was about to become engaged to the guy I had started dating at the beginning of the summer.

Finally, as I was loading my car to leave the camp, Andrew tracked me down to say good-bye. He knelt down beside me and said very sincerely, "Eva, you know how I feel about you. But I want to honor your relationship with this other guy. So I won't get in touch with you until you get in touch with me." And then he said, "But please do me a favor. Don't put a ring on your finger unless you're really sure. Please pray about it."

Well, to be honest, I was a little offended. I thought, *I go to church. I pray. I know what the Lord tells me to do. Who does this guy think he is telling me to pray about it?*

I did pray about it. The more I prayed about it, the more I realized that the guy I was dating, and to whom I became engaged, was not the right guy for me. That relationship ended up being a horrible experience. After I finally realized that this was the wrong man for me to marry, I still didn't quite know how to break off the engagement. I was twenty-eight years old. The date had already been set for the wedding. I already had my wedding dress, and my friends seemed excited that I was getting married. I finally decided that I would just tell people I was postponing the wedding for a while.

I went to the home of my friend Jeannie, and I said, "Jeannie, I've postponed the wedding." She said immediately, "Thank God."

I said, "Why did you say that?" She said, "I just think that's good, Eva."

I then blurted out, "I'm going to call it off." She said, "I think you should."

I said, "Why are you just now telling me this?" She said, "I don't know. I just don't feel right about this relationship and I haven't for quite some time."

I postponed the wedding for three months and told my fiancé to leave me alone during that time. He continued to send cards, flowers, and to call. He continually tried to manipulate my emotions and me. Finally, I called off the entire engagement and broke off the relationship.

Not long after that, in the summer of 1989, I ran into Kevin Singleton, a friend of Andrew's. In fact, Kevin was on his way to Kentucky where he and Andrew were going to speak at the same summer camp. So I gave Kevin my business card and wrote a little note on the back that said, "Dear Andrew, do you remember me? I used to be your favorite crippled FCA staffer! I still do sit-ups and bake banana nut bread."

A week later I got ten of Andrew's business cards with a *letter* written on the back of them. He began by saying, "Dear Eva, do I remember you? I've had a crush on you for years."

Months later, Becky and I moved in with my parents. After Hurricane Hugo hit our neighborhood in Charlotte, we didn't have electricity for quite some time. I had my annual FCA fund-raising dinner and I don't think we raised enough money even to cover the cost of the food for the dinner. I was still trying to get over my broken engagement and it seemed as though nothing in my life was going well.

One night, I was feeling a little down about Mama's cancer, about being single, and about living out of a suitcase. As I sat on my bed praying about life, I reached over and picked up my prayer journal. I prayed, "Lord, is it always going to be like this?" I opened the journal to a page with Andrew's name and address. I closed the book quickly and said, "Oh, Lord, where are we going with this?" It's not that I didn't like Andrew, I just didn't know what to *do* about Andrew.

A few months later, I was driving with Lynnette to an FCA retreat. I casually asked her about Andrew. She cheerfully told me that he was dating a very sweet and beautiful girl. I said, "Well, what's he dating her for?" She said, "Eva, I can't believe you! You had your chance and you blew it! I'm glad he's dating this girl." I told her I was glad, too—

but my tone of voice was a little sarcastic. I couldn't believe he was dating someone else! And I wondered if I really had blown it.

At the retreat, I was doing the music and my pastor friend Tommy Nelson was the speaker. He said to me, "Eva, Eva, I hear you're gettin' married." I said, "No, I'm not. It just wasn't right."

He said, "Eva, are you praying for a husband?" I said, "No, I just don't believe in that anymore. If God wants me to have a husband, He's going to have to send me one. I've messed it up and done it wrong all this time so He's just going to have to do it."

He said, "I'm going to put you on my prayer list. Eva. Husband. You send me an invitation." I said, "All right, Tommy." That was in February of 1990.

In April I was to speak at Icthus, a Christian festival at Asbury College in Kentucky. Andrew lived in Kentucky. I thought, *I'm going to Kentucky. I'll call Andrew.* I figured Kentucky was a pretty small state so I assumed we'd be right around the corner from each other. Andrew was too much of a gentleman to tell me that the Icthus festival was almost four hours away from where he lived!

I called Andrew at work and asked if he could call me back later when he was at home. He did, and we talked for quite some time. He asked if I was dating anybody and I said no. Then I told him that I knew he was dating someone. He acted surprised so I told him about my conversation with Lynnette.

He said, "Eva, I'm not dating her. I did go out with her and I tried to have a conversation with her, but we simply weren't on the same wavelength. She didn't understand my analogy so I knew she wasn't the right one."

I took the bait and said, "Well, what was your analogy, Andrew?"

He said, "We were talking about relationships and I told her that I wasn't looking for a date to the prom, but that I wanted somebody who would be willing to take a train ride. I told her I wasn't sure if the train was going all the way to the end of the track, but I was looking for somebody who was willing to get on board and see if it did. Eva, she didn't have any idea what I was talking about."

I said, "Really?" We went on to talk about a few other things and then the time came to end the call. Andrew asked, "So, Eva, have you ever ridden a train before?"

I started telling him about the train I had ridden when I went to England to visit friends. There was silence on his end. He finally said, "I don't think we're talking about the same thing." Then it dawned on me. I said, "Oh, I get it! I get it." He said, "Well, let me tell you what I'm talking about."

I was really embarrassed. I said, "No, Andrew, I get it." He insisted. He said, "Eva, I think if Hopkinsville and Charlotte were closer, I'd like to court you." I said, "Andrew, I think I'd like to try that train ride."

The more we talked and the more we spent time with each other, it became very apparent that the train we were riding was going all the way to the end of the track.

I have to admit I was a little slow at first. It took me a little while before I got on the right track, but the Lord, in His sovereignty, wasn't going to let me miss this "good thing." He won't let you miss the good thing He has planned for you, either.

25

n His Time

To everything there is a season,
A time for every purpose under heaven.
(Ecclesiastes 3:1)

25

*A*s our courtship became more and more serious, Andrew and I both knew that when the time was right, we would be engaged and then married. Something else was also becoming very clear to me. Whoever married Andrew would be moving to Andrew's hometown of Hopkinsville, Kentucky.

I had lived my whole life in North Carolina and had really grown to love Charlotte. One day I told my friend Jeannie how much I would miss Charlotte. Like the good friend that she is, Jeannie made it plain, "Eva, a husband is much better than Charlotte."

While I was excited that everything was moving in a very positive direction with Andrew, I was a little disappointed that I was not going to be surprised when he finally popped the question. Little did I know the lengths that he would go to to make sure that I was surprised.

Throughout our relationship, Andrew always did his best to keep things interesting. After our relationship had become fairly serious, we always tried to keep up with each other's schedules. As part of my work for FCA, I was often on the road.

Once when I flew into the small airport of Jacksonville, North Carolina, I was surprised to hear that airport personnel had been paging me. Because this is such a small airport, I yelled across the lobby to the attendant that I was Eva Whittington, the person they had been paging. She yelled back to me so that everybody else in the lobby could hear, "Ma'am, I have a very important message for you from Andrew. He said that he believes the train is going to make it all the way to the end of the track." It was one of those messages that everybody understood even though it was in code. I was a little bit embarrassed, but even more grateful that my train ride was never dull.

During the Thanksgiving holiday in 1990, Andrew flew to Charlotte to spend time with me. I was certain that he was going to ask me to marry him during that trip. Apparently I was not the only one who was certain of that. My soon-to-be mother-in-law and sister-in-law called the day after Thanksgiving to check on us and to see if anything exciting had happened. Much to my disappointment, I had nothing special to report.

That Saturday, Andrew very discreetly showed me his travel itinerary, which had him returning to Kentucky that afternoon.

When we got to the airport, I went into the lobby with him while he checked in. He told me that he had forgotten one of his bags in the car and asked me to get it while he checked his luggage. What I didn't know at that time was that Andrew had intentionally left a small bag in the car. While I went back to get it, he gave the rest of his luggage to Jeannie's husband, John, who was hiding in the shadows of the Charlotte airport.

Andrew had devised this grand plan, which he called "Operation Engagement with Destiny." He had even gone to the trouble of having his travel agent prepare a fake itinerary showing a return flight on Saturday. Andrew's actual return flight was not until the following Monday.

When I rolled back into the airport with the bag that he had forgotten, the mood was kind of somber, as it always was at the end of a visit. We huddled in the corner of the airport and prayed together as we always did. Andrew didn't want me to accompany him to his gate because it was "such a long way."

As I got ready to leave, Andrew said, "Eva, won't it be nice when we don't have to get on planes anymore to see each other—we'll just be together? When the time is right, we'll do that." I was crying—and I'm pretty sure he was tearing up, too—at the fact that he was leaving. But I was able to get a hold of myself long enough to look him squarely in the eye and say, "Andrew, the time is right." He smiled, gave me a hug, and we went our separate ways.

I went back to my car and cried most of the way home. At the same time, Andrew scrambled downstairs and hooked up with John, who quickly raced Andrew to my house.

When I finally got home, John was pulling out of my driveway. He very casually said something to me that made it seem perfectly normal for him to be there. Becky helped me out of the car when I got home and I cried, "He's gone, Becky, he's gone." She said, without much compassion or understanding, "Oh, Eva, you'll see him again soon." She wheeled me over to the side ramp to the porch and then went in the house. As I rolled up the ramp, I saw a little wooden train sitting on the porch with a ring box in the caboose. I was thrilled with the train but upset that Andrew was on his way back to Kentucky. Then Andrew jumped out of the bushes and onto the porch and said, "Hey, will you marry me?"

I began crying even harder and couldn't say a word. So Andrew said, "Is that a yes? Do we have a yes?" Somehow I was finally able to blubber, "Yes!" As Becky came out of the house to take our picture, Andrew made sure the neighbors knew, "Ladies and gentlemen, we have a yes! We have a yes!"

Needless to say, I was surprised.

Andrew and I were married on April 6, 1991, at First Baptist Church in Charlotte. Andrew's father, Dr. Ben Self, an ordained Baptist minister and college professor, performed the ceremony.

It seemed as though the Lord worked out every detail related to the wedding. Andrew and I were both blessed to have so many wonderful Christian friends and supportive families.

The only hard part was trying to decide who would be in the wedding. I told Andrew that I wanted to have bridesmaids and honorary bridesmaids. He quickly rejected that idea, saying, "We're not going to have a varsity and a junior varsity. If you're not on the varsity, you don't get in the game." So we compromised—we each had nine attendants. While I felt bad about leaving some people out, Andrew joked that he had to go out and make new friends just to have enough guys to be in our wedding.

The weekend of the wedding was a very special time for us. It was a celebration not only of our love for each other, but our love for our Lord and the many friends with whom we had been blessed.

Andrew's dad did a great job in performing the ceremony. Because so many of those attending the wedding were athletes, former athletes, coaches, and others with an athletic background, Dad used an athletic theme. The four points in his wedding sermon were: team, starter, pain, and Coach! He told us that from that day forward, we would be a *team*. We would no longer be two individuals, but rather we would be one team. He also told us that we would both be *starters* on the team, but that it is far more important to be a finisher rather than a starter.

The third point he emphasized was that throughout our life we would experience *pain*. During those times, we would need to rely on our faith, our friends, and each other as we learned to play with pain. Finally, he reminded us that we were playing for the *Coach* of all coaches and that He is the same yesterday, today, and forever. He told us to listen to our Coach.

Everything was perfect. Well, almost everything. Right after the wedding was over, my maid of honor, Elizabeth, went up to Andrew and very matter-of-factly asked him to give her his wedding band. She quickly explained that the wedding band he had on was his father's. Elizabeth had unintentionally left Andrew's wedding band in the bathroom. When she realized her mistake during the ceremony, she somehow was able to get Dad to slip his off without any of us knowing about it. Like I said, everything was perfect.

We went to a lake house about an hour from Charlotte for our honeymooon. We played tennis, went on walks, and sat on the screened porch and talked for hours. We had to come home a couple of days early because I was running a fever. I was afraid that I was developing another pressure sore.

When we finally got back to our apartment in Hopkinsville, I had to sit on the commode holding up an IV bag of warm water to run in my "sitz bath." I was crying because I thought I had ruined our honeymoon and I didn't feel very romantic or sexy sitting there on that toilet.

After he unpacked the car, Andrew came into the bathroom eating an orange Popsicle and said, "Hey, I'll hold that." He plopped down in my wheelchair and held the IV bag up in the air for me as if it were the most normal thing in the world to do on our honeymoon. Pretty soon he had me laughing and we sat there listening to the Dove Awards on television in the other room. I looked at my new husband eating an orange Popsicle and holding that IV bag and felt that I was the most blessed woman alive.

I still feel that way. When God does something in His time, it's right.

26

opkinsville

For as he thinks in his heart, so is he.
(Proverbs 23:7)

was absolutely correct about two things: one, I was very happy to be Andrew's wife, and two, I would move to Hopkinsville, Kentucky.

I realized right away that I faced some new challenges. Not only did I have to adjust to being married, but I had to adjust to living in Andrew's hometown. The Self family is well known and respected in Hopkinsville. Andrew was an all-American boy—a good student, a good athlete, and a good guy. He was on every mother's "short list" for marrying their available daughter.

At one of my bridal showers, I was introduced to a woman who said that she didn't know if she wanted to meet me because she had always hoped Andrew would marry her daughter. Another woman asked me if I realized what a catch I had landed in Andrew. I told her that I thought Andrew had landed quite a catch himself!

Hopkinsville has about 30,000 people—about the size of my hometown of Concord. The difference was that I didn't know anybody in Hopkinsville and nobody knew me. In fact I began to think my new last name was "Andrew's wife." I can't tell you how many times I was introduced as "This is Eva, Andrew's wife."

The first time I went to the grocery store by myself I came away convinced that the people there had never seen anybody in a wheelchair before. The clerks stopped what they were doing and stared at me as I rolled down the aisles. I noticed that a number of customers were also peering down the aisles to watch me as I pushed the cart to the end of the aisle, then pulled items off the shelves and put them in my lap, and then rolled to the cart to put them in it.

These grocery store trips were so stressful for me that I asked Andrew to pray with me one night before I went shopping the next day. We prayed that the people in town would get to know me and stop staring.

The next day, a little old lady, who was obviously half blind, hobbled over to me in the store and hugged me and said she was proud of me for coming to the grocery store all by myself. I was proud of her, too!

I continued to work for the Fellowship of Christian Athletes in Kentucky for the first eight months of our marriage. But I also felt that I was getting burned out. I decided to try to get a job in music education, which was the area of my college degree. While I was studying for the teacher's exam for certification in Kentucky, I got a job substitute teaching.

My certification in North Carolina was K–12 but I had always thought I'd teach high school. I did most of my substituting in one of the middle schools, however. I had forgotten just how mischievous twelve-year-old boys can be!

One afternoon after I gave the students their assignment in science class, I noticed that one of the more active boys in the class wasn't in his seat. I looked around the classroom trying to spot him but I couldn't see him anywhere. Then I looked under my teaching table and there he was, all scrunched up and laughing to himself. I asked him what he was doing and he innocently replied, "Nuthin', Mizz Self." I told him to go back to his seat and then I looked again under the table and realized why he had been laughing. He had tied my shoelaces to the table leg!

Whether it was going to the grocery store or teaching, I

learned valuable lessons those first months and years in Hopkinsville. I learned that other people respond to me based on the way I feel about myself.

If I'm embarrassed, people get embarrassed.

If I can laugh at myself, they laugh.

If I feel sorry for myself, they pity me. If I feel confident, they are comfortable.

I decided long ago that if I'm going to be a sideshow, I'm going to be a *good* sideshow! I have a new automatic carrier for my wheelchair. It unfolds on the top of my car and lets the wheelchair down to where I can reach it. It's amazing to watch. When people stare, I sometimes say, "Hey, isn't this neat?" That gives them the freedom to come over to talk and be friendly. Rather than wish they'd pay no attention, sometimes the fact that they pay attention gives me an opportunity to make a friend.

Over time, I have become more and more comfortable in my new hometown. Now when I go to the grocery store, the clerks and I know each other by our first names. They don't care what my last name is, or that I'm in a wheelchair.

How we feel about ourselves becomes how others feel about us. That's true for every person, not just a person who is paralyzed or in a wheelchair.

Jesus said it best, of course. He said, "You shall love your neighbor as yourself" (Matt. 22:39). Sometimes it's the "as yourself" that's the most challenging part of love and acceptance.

27

Abigail

*Now to Him who is able to do exceedingly
abundantly above all that we ask or think,
according to the power that works in us,
to Him be glory.*
(Ephesians 3:20–21)

There were a lot of exciting things that happened during our first few years of marriage, but nothing was more exciting than finding out that we were expecting our first child. I still remember vividly when we got the results of the home pregnancy test that indicated I was pregnant. We both cried a little—actually, I cried a lot. Andrew knelt down and we held hands and prayed for this precious gift that God was giving us.

Having lived in a wheelchair almost sixteen years, my life in the wheelchair had become pretty routine. But being pregnant and in a wheelchair was anything but routine! We had to have my chair widened four inches to make room for everything and every body. Transferring in and out of my wheelchair was much more difficult because of the extra weight. I also had major problems with incontinence, which is not uncommon during prenancy.

Although my overall health was good, we felt that I needed an obstetrician who had experience with paraplegics. A friend of mine told me about Dr. Graves at Vanderbilt Hospital, in Nashville about an hour away. I felt very comfortable with her.

One of the potential problems that occurs in some paralyzed women is called autonomic dysreflexia. The blood pressure shoots up and the situation can be fatal unless there's a direct line to the heart for delivering a blood pressure-lowering medication. Right before the anesthesiologist inserted the needle into my neck to start this line to the heart, he turned to Andrew and said in a British accent, "Do you have a strong constitution?" Andrew said, "I don't know, but I guess we're getting ready to find out!" The doctor pushed the catheter into my neck and although he told me it would feel like a bee sting, it most certainly did *not* feel like a bee sting.

Although my legs are paralyzed, my abdomen is not. I could feel my baby kicking inside me and I could feel labor pains. I was able to push for a normal delivery for my baby. Andrew discovered he had such a strong constitution that he was able to tell lawyer jokes in the delivery room—to everyone's amusement but mine!

Abigail May Self was born after about eight hours of fairly easy labor. She was six pounds, fourteen ounces, and had auburn hair. She was absolutely perfect. Andrew cut the umbilical cord and we cried for a long time. I called Mama right away to tell her that Abigail had just arrived. She kept exclaiming, "Praise the Lord! Praise the Lord!"

Abigail May was named for Mama in more ways than one. The story of Abigail is my favorite story in the Bible. (See 1 Sam. 25.) I have often wondered if Abigail became who she was *because* of Nabal. So many women that I meet are like Abigail. They are living with men like Nabal who are abusive in some way, or men like Nabal who fail to make wise decisions that impact their families. Abigail was an *overcomer*. She found a way to bring something good out of a potentially disastrous situation. Mama was like that. She had lived with a Nabal and had overcome her situation.

As you might imagine, I had a number of concerns about being a mother. I was concerned about whether I would be able to care for my baby properly, and I wondered how I would pick up my child when she started to crawl and how I would reach my child if she started to run away from me. Somehow things have worked out. My daughter has a way of reaching me, or I have a way of reaching her.

Because I can't walk, I couldn't do some things for my child that other mothers could do. When Abby fell asleep in my arms as I rocked her in my rocking chair, I couldn't stand up, walk over to her crib, and gently lay her in it. I had to transfer her into her bouncy seat, transfer out of the rocking chair into my wheelchair, then put her into my lap in a sitting-up position, roll over to her crib, and put her into it. Somehow Abby adapted and was able to sleep through the entire process. Isn't God good?

One of my favorite things was to take Abby out for walks. Instead of pushing her in a stroller, I held her against my body and slowly rolled my wheelchair up and down the sidewalks of our neighborhood. I'd use two bandannas to tie her to my waist so that she was "belted in" safely, and off we'd go.

Although Abby knows that all moms aren't in wheel-chairs, she seems comfortable with the fact that her mom is. We do some things a little bit differently from other moms and children, but it seems natural to her.

I feel certain that the day will come, someday, when Abby will be embarrassed. I shared this with a friend one day and she said, "Oh, she'll be embarrassed by you all right, but it won't have anything to do with your chair. It will be simply because you are her mother and she's a teenager!"

After Abby was born, I also had opportunities open up for ministry again. This time they came in the form of my leading a young women's Bible study at church. I really needed the fellowship. It also made me realize that God could use a stay-at-home mom. Together, we women remind one another that the day-to-day tasks of being a mother and a wife have great significance.

I also had another unique opportunity when I heard from a good friend, Lisa Harper, who was working at the time as the director of women's ministry for Focus on the Family. Lisa had been on staff with FCA in Tennessee while I was working for FCA in North Carolina. During that time, she invited me to speak at many of her schools, and we worked together at a number of camps and retreats. She called me to ask me to share my story with women across the nation.

This was a very exciting time in my life. The Lord had given me an opportunity to minister to my young daughter, to women in my community, and to women across the country. Looking back, I realize that the Lord used these experiences to prepare me to minister to one particular woman—May Bell, my mama.

28

Saved at Last

Let us not grow weary while doing good,
for in due season we shall reap if we do not lose heart.
(Galatians 6:9)

Andrew and I talked to Mama and Daddy every Sunday to check on them. I was worried about Mama, especially when she started going to the hospital more frequently to have fluid drained from her lungs. When I asked her what the doctor had said to her on her last visit with him, Mama usually got confused and gave me vague answers.

One time when I called Mama, she was in the hospital. She seemed worse than usual but she couldn't tell me what the doctor had said to her, so I decided to call her doctor and talk to him directly. The nurse who answered the phone told me the doctor couldn't give me any details without Mama's consent so I told her I'd call Mama and then she'd call him to give consent. The nurse said, "Hold on a minute" and before I knew it, the doctor was on the phone. He said, "Mrs. Self, what exactly do you need to know?" I said, "I need to know my mama's condition." He gave me a fairly long explanation, most of which I didn't understand. I finally interrupted and said, "Doctor, I need to know if I should come home. I need to know if my Mama is dying." He said, "You need to come home."

It was two days before Easter. I felt I needed to go, even though it meant missing Abby's first Easter egg hunt.

I flew to Charlotte and went to the house to pick up Daddy and then together we drove straight to the hospital. Mama perked up when I rolled into her room and she said with a grin, "Here's my daughter!" After visiting for a while, I gently told her that the doctors didn't think she'd live much longer. She took a minute to process everything and then with tears streaming down her face, she looked at me and said, "May His will be done, Eva. May His will be done."

Daddy was pretty quiet when we left the hospital. I wasn't sure whether he didn't understand what was going on, or if he was just pretending not to understand. I knew we needed to start making some arrangements to prepare for Mama's death but Daddy just wasn't "with it."

When I got up the next morning, Easter Sunday, I noticed that Daddy was all dressed up. To my surprise, he told me he thought we should go to church. I said, "That's all right with me, and I think Mama would like that, Daddy." I was thankful that Daddy wanted to be in church on Easter, or on any day for that matter! I called Mama at the hospital and told her we'd come by and see her after church. She seemed excited, too, that Daddy and I were going to church.

We went to Broadus Memorial Baptist Church. My brother Ted was a member there—he had become a Christian about a year earlier. Daddy had been attending fairly regularly with Ted and Mama for several months because he liked the preacher, Rodney Quesenberry. Rodney was an old high school friend of mine—in fact, he had been the quarterback of the football team when I was a cheerleader. I knew God must have really changed Rodney's life for him to be a pastor. I also knew that two of the reasons Daddy liked to hear Rodney preach were because he talked in simple, practical, everyday terms and because he talked real *loud*. Daddy liked that because he could hear every word Rodney said.

At the end of the service, Rodney gave an invitation to accept Christ. He said that it was never too late to enter the kingdom of God, even if a person was eighty years old. He said that some people needed to come down front and then he suggested that we offer to walk down the aisle with the person sitting next to us. Ted looked at me and then turned to Daddy and said, "Pap, do you want me . . ." Ted couldn't even finish the question before Daddy stepped out and headed down the aisle. He walked straight toward Rodney and Rodney walked up the aisle to meet him. When he got to Rodney, he took his hand and knelt down. At the age of eighty, my daddy finally gave his life to Jesus Christ.

There were times before that day in which I asked the Lord to take Daddy on home if He wasn't going to save him because Daddy was obviously miserable and he was making the rest of us miserable, too. But all the while, God was softening Daddy's heart little by little. It was an amazing day. My daddy got saved!

Ted couldn't hold back the news. He called Mama at the hospital even before we got there that afternoon. When we walked into her room, she was sitting up in bed grinning. Daddy said, "Mom, I've got something to tell you." She said, "Ted done told me and I just started yelling. Them nurses come in here and wanted to know what all the fuss was about and I tol' them my husband just got saved!"

Daddy was crying and he walked over and hugged her and said, "Now we won't ever be apart."

I had flown to North Carolina thinking that I was going to tell Mama good-bye, but I realized that God had graciously allowed me to go home so that I could see my daddy finally commit his life to Jesus Christ.

Every person is either like my mama or my daddy—you are either praying for somebody, or somebody is praying for you. If you are praying for somebody, don't give up! Mama prayed for Daddy for more than forty years. I prayed in earnest for Daddy for more than fifteen years. There were lots of times when I wanted to give up, but the Lord encouraged me again and again to keep praying. After all, Mama had been praying far longer than I had been, and she hadn't given up.

You may have been praying for someone for a long time. Don't stop. As James wrote, "The effective, fervent prayer of a righteous man avails much" (James 5:16).

If you are not like my mama—praying for someone—you may be like my daddy and somebody is praying for you. It may be a family member, a friend, or somebody you don't even know. God has a timetable. He has a plan for *your* life. If prayer could be answered in my daddy's life, it can be answered in *anybody's* life, including yours.

Is today the day for you to surrender *your* life to Jesus Christ?

29

Audrey

Eye has not seen, nor ear heard,
Nor have entered into the heart of man
The things which God has prepared for
those who love Him.
(1 Corinthians 2:9)

On the Friday before Mother's Day 1995, I called Mama and put Abby on the phone. Mama loved listening to Abby "talk." Mama, however, could barely talk that day and I knew in my heart she was slipping away. I was scheduled to speak that day at a Mother's Day program at a retirement home and it was probably the most difficult talk I've ever given. I knew Mama was dying while I was speaking.

When I got home, I jumped every time the phone rang. Daddy finally called and said he had just heard from the hospital. The nurse had said Mama would probably die within the hour. I had been crying all afternoon, mainly because I couldn't be at the hospital with Mama. But once Daddy told me she only had an hour left, I felt thankful, somehow, that God was merciful to let me know the moment she crossed over into glory. I could pray for her, at least, as she was meeting Jesus face-to-face.

Mama's pastor, Rodney, was with her when she died and he told us later that several times during the last hour of her life, Mama raised both hands over her head and a huge smile spread across her face. Rodney tried to get her to tell him what she was seeing or experiencing, but she couldn't. She just smiled and raised her hands as if she were a little girl and her father was reaching down to pick her up.

I believe that's exactly what happened.

I missed Mama terribly after she died. I was constantly reminded of little things she said and did, and I mourned the fact that Abby would never really know her. One day I called home because I needed her help with a recipe—I instinctively dialed her number and it was only when the phone started to ring that I realized she wasn't going to answer and that we'd never talk on the phone again.

We continued to call Daddy on Sundays and soon, it became apparent that he wasn't doing very well physically or emotionally. The fact was, Daddy had lung cancer, too. Within a few months, he was bedridden and we drove back and forth several times to help him and to arrange for his care.

Pastor Rodney and another friend from church, Rina, were the only two people outside of family members whom Daddy trusted. Rodney was faithful in coming by to visit Daddy every couple of days. He'd pray with him and listen to Daddy tell his same stories again and again. Rina would come by with her three boys. She brought Daddy food and made him eat it while she was sitting there. Her boys would crawl all over Daddy and tell him their stories about baseball and T-ball. There's a song that says, "They'll know we are Christians by our love." I have no doubt whatsoever that Rodney and Rina are Christians.

Rodney was with Daddy, too, when he died—fourteen months to the day after Mama was buried. Like Mama, Daddy kept pointing at the ceiling and smiling in the hours before he slipped away. I like to think of Daddy as being like the thief on the cross when Jesus was crucified. God mercifully granted salvation to Daddy at the very end of his life.

Rodney told me that a couple of months before Daddy died, Daddy had prayed with Rodney. The prayer had actually been Daddy's idea. He said to the Lord, "I haven't asked You to forgive me for *all* of my sins. I'm asking You now to forgive me for *all* my sins." Rodney said Daddy seemed to have a lot more peace after he prayed that prayer. I did, too, when Rodney told me.

Six months after Daddy's death, I became pregnant with our second child. We had been trying for almost two years to get pregnant and I had just about concluded that it wasn't ever going to happen. But then, as if God chose to bless us with a new life after calling Mama and Daddy home, Audrey came along.

Audrey Carolyn Self was born on October 10, 1997. She was named after Andrew's mom, Carolyn, and Andrew's grandmother, Audrie—two godly women.

Some of the things I'm trying to "just do" for my daughters are things I realize Mama did for me.

I want to live the life of a Christian, not just talk about it.

I want to teach my girls by my example that it really doesn't matter how bad things are, or how bad things get, Christ meets us where we are. In some way, He can bring good out of any situation—somewhere, somehow, and at some time, if not in this life, in the next.

I want my daughters to grow up knowing that their mother prays and trusts God, and that they can pray and trust God for themselves.

I have a long "wish" list for my children when I pray for them. But when it's all said and done, I also pray, "Lord, *if* they have to go through bad things in order to know You better, then Your will be done." Nothing matters as much as knowing the Lord.

If my daughters learn those lessons, I will be pleased. I know Mama would be pleased. But most important, I know my heavenly Father will be pleased.

30

Treasures Old and New

But we have this treasure in earthen vessels,
that the excellence of the power
may be of God and not of us.
(2 Corinthians 4:7)

$\mathcal{A}$ month after Daddy's funeral, Becky flew into Charlotte and met my mother-in-law, Carolyn, and me. We then drove to Concord to clean out Mama and Daddy's house. Several of my brothers had already taken mementos that were important to them. All I really wanted was Mama's old cedar chest. Ever since I was a little girl, I had known the cedar chest at the foot of Mama's bed housed all kinds of special secrets.

Mama was something of a pack rat so it took the three of us a day and a half to sift through and clean out the things she had accumulated in the house. When the last box was packed, we pulled the cedar chest out into the living room to sort through its contents.

The cedar chest was filled with treasures—no stock certificates or anything of monetary value, but treasures all the same. There was a baby book with the name of Mama's first child, a little girl named Geraldine, who was stillborn. There was a bundle of love letters that Mama and Daddy wrote to each other before they were married. They addressed each other as "Honey" and "Darling" throughout the letters. I had never heard them call each other by those names and they were never very affectionate around me. It made me smile to think of them as young sweethearts.

I realized from the letters that Daddy had actually quit playing baseball so he could marry Mama. That was special to me.

I also found pictures of Mama in the back of her photo album. She had a horribly bruised face and one of her eyes was swollen shut. She had bruises on her neck, too. I knew they were pictures of the time when Mama had been raped.

I kept the things in that cedar chest and when the time is right, I will tell my girls more about their grandmother. I *am* May Bell's daughter. They'll understand me better the more they know about Mama.

But the fact is also that they are May Bell's granddaughters. And my prayer is that they will love the Lord as much as their grandmother did. The Lord was the most important person in the world to Mama. And I pray the Lord will also be the most important person in the world to Abby and Audrey. If He is, their lives will be full and rich *forever*.

Recently, Andrew and I flew into Charlotte for a speaking engagement. We rented a car and drove to Concord while we were in the area. When we turned onto Linden Avenue, my heart started racing a little as we got closer to our old house. Someone else lives there now.

We parked across the street in the church parking lot and I noticed the two dogwood trees I had given Mama and Daddy several years before they died. They were already blooming. We drove to the cemetery where Mama and Daddy were buried. There was a new headstone next to them marking Geraldine's grave.

As we stood there in the cemetery, I found myself telling Mama that I was going to speak in the Greensboro Coliseum the next day and I wished she could be there to see it. I longed to go home and walk into the backyard and find her picking tomatoes.

The next day I had the opportunity to share my story with more than 16,000 women at Focus on the Family's "Renewing the Heart Conference" in the Greensboro

Coliseum. There were four twenty-foot screens suspended above the stage projecting our images to the audience. Giant clusters of speakers were suspended on thick metal cables from the ceiling of the arena. Spotlights flooded the stage and television and newspaper reporters scrambled for good camera angles. It was a lot different from the first time I had shared my testimony there almost twenty years earlier.

As I wheeled out onto that stage, I realized how much had happened to me in the last twenty years of my life. I had graduated from college, worked for a ministry, married, buried two parents, and given birth to two beautiful little girls.

I realized that I had "walked" in places Mama never got to go. I had seen and experienced things she could only have dreamed about. But I also realized that her legacy of faith is what had given me both a foundation that was firm and wings to soar. I realized that in all those years God had been faithful, and faithfulness is the one thing Mama had always known about the Lord.

It's the only thing that's really important for me to share with you. My life is just an *example*. The real message is Jesus and what He can do in any person's life, including yours.

He loves you.

He has always loved you and He *will* always love you.

He has a plan and a purpose for your life.

He longs to forgive you and to be in a walk-and-talk relationship with you every day for as long as you live.

And He will be faithful to you always.

I don't have a single doubt about it.

I learned these truths from a simple woman. Her name was May Bell. I am May Bell's daughter.